Computer Science for Kids

Computer Science for Kids

A Storytelling Approach

Jen Looper

WILEY

To all the kids who don't see themselves as having a place in Computer Science . . . Remember that your story is yet to be told!

About the Author

 **Jen Looper** is the Head of Academic Advocacy at AWS, previously at Microsoft, and a Google Developer Expert with over 22 years' experience as a web and mobile developer, specializing in creating cross-platform mobile and web apps. With a PhD in medieval French literature, Jen is a multilingual multiculturalist with a passion for web technologies and applied machine learning, and for discovering new things every day. Her area of focus is curriculum development and the application of sound pedagogy to technical topics. A lecturer in computer science at Boston University's Metropolitan College, she is also the founder and CEO of Front-End Foxes, Inc., an international nonprofit charity that promotes diversity in front-end developer communities. Visit Jen at www.jenlooper.com or connect via Twitter @jenlooper.

About the Technical Editors

Andrea Russo is the Field Enablement and Go to Market Lead for the Microsoft Philanthropies Digital Inclusion Program. She has worked for the program for the past six years. When she started as a regional manager, her role was co-funded by Governor Gina Raimondo's CS4RI initiative through 2018. While Andrea was in that role, Rhode Island became the first state to offer computer science opportunities to every public school in the state and received Harvard's Innovation in Government Award. Before joining Technology Education and Literacy in Schools, Andrea worked for the National Council of Technological Literacy and taught grades 6–12 in New York City as a STEM teacher. Prior to her teaching career, she worked at the New York Botanical Garden in the Continuing Education department. She holds an M.S. and an M.Ed.

Chris Noring is a Senior Cloud Advocate at Microsoft. He's been in the IT industry for more than 15 years and has worked on multiple tech stacks as well as front- and backend. Chris is a community organizer and co-creator of the Angular conference ngVikings, and is a published author on the JavaScript framework Angular as well as the Go language.

Justin Leonard is a middle school educator with Prince George County Public Schools, Maryland. In his current role, he is a Project Lead the Way (PLTW) Gateway instructor. He also teaches graduate-level courses for the Master of Arts in Education in the STEM Education program at the University of Maryland, Baltimore County.

Acknowledgments

I'd like to acknowledge the many readers of drafts of this book, including Mrs. Gentes's eighth-grade computer science students at Wellesley Middle School. Thanks also go to Wellesley High School's Dr. Cohen, always a helpful teacher, who has listened to many of my wild ideas with interest and has given me useful feedback. Thank you to Allegra Hu, who created the prototype of the Guide as a cloaked fox figure. Illustrations are by Mirla Montaño. I'd like to thank my patient editors and hardworking technical reviewers. I'd above all like to thank my family for their encouragement in writing this book.

Contents

Introduction

When you think about computer science, what pops into your head? Someone crouched over a computer, typing code all night long? Someone in a room full of computers, messing around with wires? Someone solving long mathematical equations by writing a lot of hard-to-understand computer programs? Does that person look like you?

What if you thought about computer science in a different way—as a way to solve mysteries? Isn't it more fun to think about yourself as an intrepid explorer, out to solve challenging puzzles by writing clever bits of software? Can you see yourself as the hero or heroine of a story, ready to slay the dragons of slow, buggy, hard-to-read software and make the world a little more pleasant by means of great user design and well-functioning programs?

In this book, you'll be given the opportunity to become a helper—someone who is able to solve challenges by writing computer programs. Summoned by a mysterious figure who emerges from a forest and asks for your help, you are invited to participate in a series of tasks to make this forest a little safer and more hospitable for its native inhabitants.

Are you up to the task?

Computer Science Teachers Association Standards

This book is structured using the Computer Science Teachers Association standards for Grades 6–8, covering ages 11–14. These standards are available at `https://csteachers.org`. In general, they are arranged around five concepts:

- Algorithms & Programming
- Computing Systems
- Data & Analysis
- Impacts of Computing
- Networks & the Internet

The standards help shape the projects that are used to drive home general concepts of computer science. This is not a book about programming languages, however. Rather than diving deep into JavaScript and Python, we focus on the standards that teach general concepts of computer science. The projects in each chapter are designed to be part of an evolving story line, rather than teaching a language in depth. A good computer scientist will eventually become skilled in many programming languages, however, so it's a good idea to pair this book with study of Python or JavaScript.

Although the book is structured to these standards, the content has not been reviewed, validated, or endorsed by CSTA.

Each chapter includes a story line, suggestions for angles to research, a "Think Like a Computer Scientist" section to introduce computer science concepts, a sketch of a project, a Project Recipe with detailed instructions on how to create a project to illustrate the computer science concept, a vocabulary review, a final quiz to help emphasize concepts, and an assignment. All the projects can be built in a web browser using free and open source tools, so you won't need any special installations or downloads to get started. This book can be used for self-study, as a textbook for homeschoolers, or in a classroom. Use it chapter by chapter, piece by piece, or section by section for a more modular learning experience.

What Does This Book Cover?

In the five sections of this book, you'll discover many aspects of computer science, presented as project-based stories:

Part I: The Missing Fireflies – Using Microsoft micro:bit in a browser emulator, create a home for runaway fireflies.

Chapter 1: The Trapper

Chapter 2: The Firefly Refuge

Chapter 3: The Fireflies' Message

Chapter 4: A Home for All

Part II: The Glowing Moss – Save the endangered moss by building a gamified enclosure for them using Microsoft MakeCode.

Chapter 5: Goblins' Gold

Chapter 6: Securing the Moss

Chapter 7: The Whisper Network

Chapter 8: A Well-Tested Solution

Part III: Geode Quest – Conserve the rare geodes hidden in the riverbed by using data science techniques to categorize the forest's inventory of stones.

Chapter 9: Searching for Geodes

Chapter 10: Cleaning and Categorizing the Collection

Chapter 11: The Stone Library

Chapter 12: Hide or Seek

Part IV: The Petrified Forest – Protect the fragile petrified wood in the forest grove by visualizing a 3D environment to simulate their preservation.

Chapter 13: The Petrified Forest

Chapter 14: The Butterfly Brigade

Chapter 15: Power of the Weak

Chapter 16: The Written Artifact

Part V: Legends of the Field Mice – Using Twine, a free tool to tell winding stories, help the field mice unlock the secret of their underground realm.

Chapter 17: The Field Mice

Chapter 18: Lights, Sounds, Action

Chapter 19: Unlocking the Vault

Chapter 20: The Real World

Additional Resources

This textbook is paired with a full website found at `https://cs4kids.club`. This website includes a kids' section called Quests with links to completed sample projects on MakeCode, GitHub, and Twine. Worksheets can also be found that can be used to complete assignments. There's also a teacher's section with full lesson plans, answers to quizzes, differentiated learning suggestions, and more resources for each chapter's topic.

Standards Map

Table I.1 includes a map of standards covered within this book along with the chapters where each appear.

TABLE I.1 Standards mapping

Identifier	Standard	Chapter
2-CS-01	Recommend improvements to the design of computing devices, based on an analysis of how users interact with the devices.	2
2-CS-02	Design projects that combine hardware and software components to collect and exchange data.	1
2-CS-03	Systematically identify and fix problems with computing devices and their components.	3
2-NI-04	Model the role of protocols in transmitting data across networks and the Internet.	5
2-NI-05	Explain how physical and digital security measures protect electronic information.	6
2-NI-06	Apply multiple methods of encryption to model the secure transmission of information.	7
2-DA-07	Represent data using multiple encoding schemes.	9
2-DA-08	Collect data using computational tools and transform the data to make it more useful and reliable.	10
2-DA-09	Refine computational models based on the data they have generated.	11
2-AP-10	Use flowcharts and/or pseudocode to address complex problems as algorithms.	13
2-AP-11	Create clearly named variables that represent different data types and perform operations on their values.	14
2-AP-12	Design and iteratively develop programs that combine control structures, including nested loops and compound conditionals.	15
2-AP-13	Decompose problems and subproblems into parts to facilitate the design, implementation, and review of programs.	17
2-AP-14	Create procedures with parameters to organize code and make it easier to reuse.	18
2-AP-15	Seek and incorporate feedback from team members and users to refine a solution that meets user needs.	19
2-AP-16	Incorporate existing code, media, and libraries into original programs, and give attribution.	13
2-AP-17	Systematically test and refine programs using a range of test cases.	8

Identifier	Standard	Chapter
2-AP-18	Distribute tasks and maintain a project timeline when collaboratively developing computational artifacts.	17,18
2-AP-19	Document programs in order to make them easier to follow, test, and debug.	16
2-IC-20	Compare tradeoffs associated with computing technologies that affect people's everyday activities and career options.	20
2-IC-21	Discuss issues of bias and accessibility in the design of existing technologies.	4
2-IC-22	Collaborate with many contributors through strategies such as crowdsourcing or surveys when creating a computational artifact.	17
2-IC-23	Describe tradeoffs between allowing information to be public and keeping information private and secure.	12

How to Contact Wiley or the Author

Contact the author using the Contact Us form at `https://cs4kids.club`.

If you believe you have found a mistake in this book, please bring it to our attention. At John Wiley & Sons, we understand how important it is to provide our customers with accurate content, but even with our best efforts an error may occur.

To submit your possible errata, please email them to our Customer Service Team at `wileysupport@wiley.com` with the subject line "Possible Book Errata Submission."

Preface

It's a steamy summer evening, and you struggle to concentrate on the pages of your math homework. The curtains hanging over your open window are completely motionless, as not a breath of air stirs the murky twilight. You gaze out into the gathering darkness, not thinking about anything other than whether you have the energy to walk downstairs to get another cool drink of water. Outside, the steady buzz-buzz-buzz of cicadas starts to thrum through the dusk, and as the darkness intensifies, you notice a pinpoint of light twinkling fitfully in the woods outside your house. Normally, you only visit the forest in the daytime, where you enjoy watching insects and animals go about their daily business. They always seem busy and happy, and you like observing their habits with your handy binoculars and magnifying glass that help you watch both birds and tiny bugs.

Tonight, however, the forest is strangely dark, except for that feebly flickering light. Even though your room is too warm for comfort, you feel a cold shiver down your spine. What is that light? It doesn't look like the fireflies that usually swirl merrily in the dark, flashing their gaudy yellow, white, and sometimes green luminescence. Tonight, the forest has faded to black. Have all the fireflies left? Are their glows concentrated in that one pinpoint of light? Giving up on trying to concentrate on your homework, you decide to investigate.

Rummaging through your drawer of handy tools, you grab your explorer kit containing a flashlight, some bug spray, a pad of paper and a pencil, and other random things such as a spare shoelace, an extra battery, and a stick of gum. Leaning cautiously out of your window, you shine your flashlight into the blackness, but, as you noticed before, there is no friendly flicker of a firefly to twinkle and light up the night. Where have they gone? And why does that flickering light seem to be pulsing in a pattern now? Is it a code that you need to decipher?

· · · · − − − · · ·

You recognize the old Morse code signal: "S.O.S." It stands for Save Our Ship, and it's a distress signal! Three short flashes, three long flashes, three short flashes. Something is definitely wrong. It's time to investigate.

1
The Missing Fireflies

1. The Trapper

Standard: 2-CS-02: Understand how to design a project that combines hardware and software components that collect and work with data

Equipped with your explorer paraphernalia, you boldly walk toward the pulsing light. Crunching through underbrush, you watch as the light becomes brighter as you approach it. Soon, you see that it's a lantern, held by . . . a cloaked figure.

You stop short as it turns to face you. Removing its hood, it is revealed to be a figure resembling a fox. Her eyes glow with a green luminescence and she raises her lantern. "Welcome, explorer," she says quietly. "Are you here to help restore this sacred space, or are you yet another one who pillages, steals, and destroys?"

Assuring the figure of your good intentions, you ask how you can help. She responds, "I'm sure you noticed how dark the forest has become. I have come to seek help in restoring the fireflies to their rightful home. Are you up to the task?"

You're quite sure that, given the right technology, you can create some kind of hardware system that will attract fireflies back to their home. You decide to build a firefly trapper gadget to make them return to the forest. Maybe, by creating a machine that mimics the flash patterns of different types of fireflies, you can attract the insects to the Trapper.

> Note
>
> Depending on where you're from, you might call fireflies "lightning bugs." They have many other names; in Jamaica they are called "blinkies" or "peenie wallies." Their larvae are sometimes called "glow worms."

Do Some Research

Can you build a firefly trap to capture fireflies and discover their secrets? Learn a bit about fireflies and their habits, as well as what attracts them, and you can design a firefly trapper using MakeCode's micro:bit in the emulator or, if you have it, on a real device. Your task is to use your device emulator to simulate the flashing patterns of fireflies as they try to attract mates.

Note

MakeCode and micro:bit are free tools that we'll be using in this section to build device designs and games. MakeCode (`https://arcade.makecode.com`) has an "arcade" where you can develop simple 2D games, and micro:bit (`https://makecode.microbit.org`) helps you build hardware systems that sense, blink, and react to their surroundings. Micro:bit works both in the emulator, an online environment that simulates a real hardware device, and on its own hardware, which you can purchase online if you want. For this book, you aren't required to buy micro:bits, but they are fun gadgets to own!

All the chapters in this book use tools that work in the browser. You can develop and save your work right in your web browser as long as you have an Internet connection. To preserve your work, you can download a copy from your online browser session, or, better yet, upload a copy to GitHub if you have an account there. GitHub is a place that allows you to store your work.

According to the National Park Service, different fireflies flash various colors and patterns, depending on their type. Can you copy the pattern shown in Figure 1.1 using a micro:bit to attract a firefly?

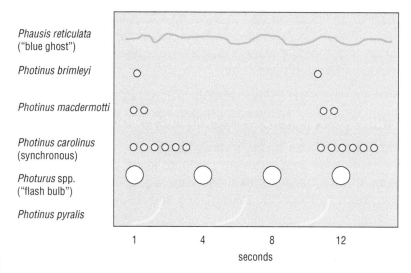

FIGURE 1.1: The National Park Service's comparison of flash patterns of fireflies in the Great Smoky Mountains Park

Your research leads you to focus on the interplay between male and female fireflies. A particular species of firefly, *Photinus brimleyi,* has an interesting pattern of communication that you can try to copy:

- The males of this species flash yellow light at intervals of 10 seconds or longer.
- Females respond to the male's light flash with a single flash from the forest floor.

You surmise that if two fireflies flash their lights at the same time, you can consider it a "match" and the attraction will succeed—at least, that is your hypothesis.

Sketch It Out

Draw a quick paper sketch of the elements you need to build your prototype. It's a hardware project, but fortunately you don't actually need hardware to accomplish it. This challenge will allow you to learn how to prototype, or make a model of, interesting software projects using *blocks*, visual representations of your software that snap together like puzzle pieces. You can do this in a web browser using MakeCode's micro:bit emulator.

The micro:bit emulator also includes Python and JavaScript tabs if you want to jump right into writing code rather than using blocks. For this prototype, however, you can use blocks. Don't worry if you don't know Python or JavaScript for the projects in this book. These programming languages, which are used to build websites and work with data, are very useful to know but they are not covered in depth here. To dive deeper into these languages, you can use the many free online tools, such as `FreeCodeCamp.org` and `Code.org`.

Since you need to create a device that simulates the colored flashing lights of male and female fireflies, and the basic micro:bit device only has a few LED lights available as built-in lights and they can only flash red light, you need to add two "strips" of LEDs that will act like the fireflies.

Definition

Light-emitting diodes (LEDs) are a semiconductor light source that uses less power to emit light than a conventional incandescent bulb, and so are often used in low-power applications.

Draw a sketch of your device with two LED strips connected to the micro:bit and the score displayed on the built-in LED display. Your sketch might look something like Figure 1.2.

Your Challenge

Your job is to design a program that will:

- Reproduce a sequence of yellow male light flashes that appear every 10 seconds

8

- Generate random flashes of white light to reproduce the female flash
- Create a system whereby if a female flash happens at the same time as a male flash, a "match" can be made (in your case, a point tallied)

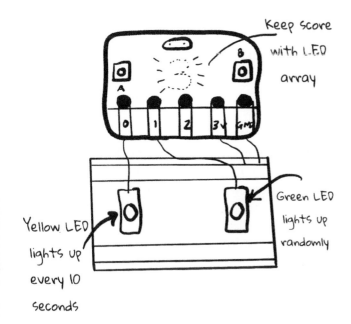

Keep score with LED array

Yellow LED lights up every 10 seconds

Green LED lights up randomly

FIGURE 1.2: A sketch of how your device might look

With this plan, or software specification, in hand, you are ready to build a prototype of your firefly trapper using blocks, right in the MakeCode micro:bit emulator.

Think Like a Computer Scientist: Design Your System

Your task is to design a project that combines hardware and software components to collect and exchange information. What does that look like? Imagine you are designing a device that can collect the temperature from a sensor.

You need to take those temperature readings and store them on a computer somewhere, perhaps in the cloud.

In the real world, computer scientists and information technology professionals need to think about the systems that must be designed to solve a problem such as this one. They would need to consider the machinery, or hardware, needed to gather temperature readings, as well as the computer programs, or software, to store this information. Consider the hardware requirements for this type of system: what machinery would you choose to gather information and send it from sensor to server? Would the device collecting the temperature data need to be physically plugged into an electrical source, or could it get its power a different way, such as through a solar panel?

Now, consider this system's software requirements. How would your hardware connect to the server to send information for storage? Sensors that gather information minute by minute often send a lot of data to the cloud, where it can be stored to be reviewed later. The more data you need to store, the more you might have to pay for that storage. You might want to plan to store a lot of data, or just a part of your data, depending on how long you want to keep it and how much of it you really need.

Think about trade-offs that you need to make when designing this system that combines hardware and software. You might, for example, need to think about how much it will cost to make sure that the various parts of the system remain functional and how to manage those costs. If an element is particularly fragile, for example, perhaps it could be replaced with something better suited to the environment it inhabits. This device needs to work outside, so it probably should be relatively robust and be protected from the elements. In the real world, computer scientists need to think about their systems as a whole and manage failure scenarios, costs, data management, and more. Your task right now is to think on a systems level and build a basic model of a machine combining hardware and software that can attract the missing fireflies.

Project Recipe

Go to `https://makecode.microbit.org` and click New Project. Give your project a name, something like **firefly trapper**. As you work in the micro:bits emulator, your project will be saved in the browser, although you can also download a copy of the project and run it on an actual micro:bit device if you have one. Don't worry if you don't.

Step 1: Import the Neopixel Extension and Connect Two Neopixels to the Micro:bit

In your new project, locate the center panel where the controls are. Scroll to the Advanced area at the bottom and expand this panel to reveal Extensions. Click the Extensions button and search for Neopixel. Import the Neopixel extension to your project by clicking the tile. Once imported, the Neopixel extension becomes part of your project. If you click the Neopixel tab in the center panel, as shown in Figure 1.3, you will see the blocks it provides. You can connect these fancy strips of LEDs to your micro:bit.

Drag a red `set strip` block into your project and clip it into the `on start` element (called the `on start` block) that is on your project screen. Click the drop-down labeled strip and scroll to the bottom to create a new variable. Call the new variable `maleLights`. You can keep the pin drop-down at its default value, P0. Set the number of LEDs to **3** to keep the view of the strip short. You'll learn more details about variables in the next section.

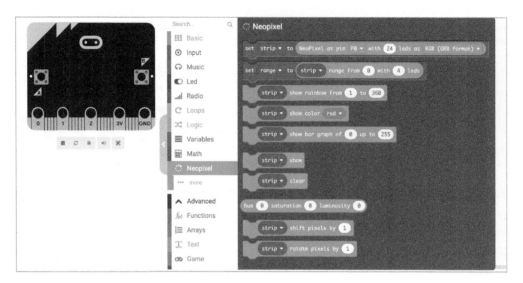

FIGURE 1.3: The Neopixel panel

> **Note**
>
> If you make a mistake while dragging blocks around the screen, you can drag a block to the left to delete it. A trash can icon in the center panel indicates a place to discard stray blocks.

Duplicate this strip in the `on start` block to build the female lights simulation by right-clicking the first strip (you can also use your keyboard to duplicate a block by pressing Ctrl+C to copy followed by Ctrl+V to paste). Create a new variable in the same way as before, but this time call it `femaleLights`. Use the pin drop-down to attach this strip to the P0 pin and the `femaleLights` strip to P1, so that the two strips are now shown on a simulated breadboard, as you can see in Figure 1.4.

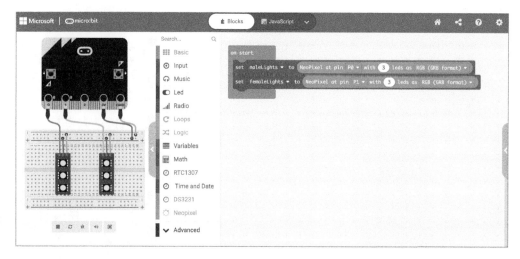

FIGURE 1.4: The first two blocks

Definition

In the micro:bit emulator, you notice that the actual device is connected to LED strips that are attached to a *breadboard*, a rectangular board with lots of labeled holes. A breadboard is a device that allows you to connect various elements to power supplies and sensors.

Definition

In programming, a *variable* is a named storage container that can be assigned and sometimes reassigned a value. A variable named `pet` can be assigned to the string, a type of data used for text, that might be "cat," "dog," or "fish." A variable named `price` can be set to the number 1.50 or 100.

Step 2: Create *on start* Variables

Next, you need to create some more variables. Open the Variables panel and create a new variable named **score**, as shown in Figure 1.5. Notice that when you create this variable, a new set and change block is created, as shown in Figure 1.5. Drag the `Set Score to 0` block into the project window and clip it into the `on start` block at the end.

FIGURE 1.5: Making a new variable

Create two more new variables in this panel and call them **yellowLit** and **greenLit**. Duplicate the `Set Score` block twice and change the drop-down to **yellowLit** and **greenLit**, respectively. These two variables will be Booleans, which means they can only have the value of `true` or `false`. Clip these blocks into the `on start` block.

Go to the Logic panel and scroll to the bottom. Drag a `false` diamond into the workspace. Clip that into the `set greenLit` block by connecting the red circles that appear when you drag the Boolean element toward the `Set` block. Duplicate that Boolean and drag it into the `set yellowLit` block in the same way. Now you've built your `on start` block so that your interface is ready for display. It looks like Figure 1.6.

14

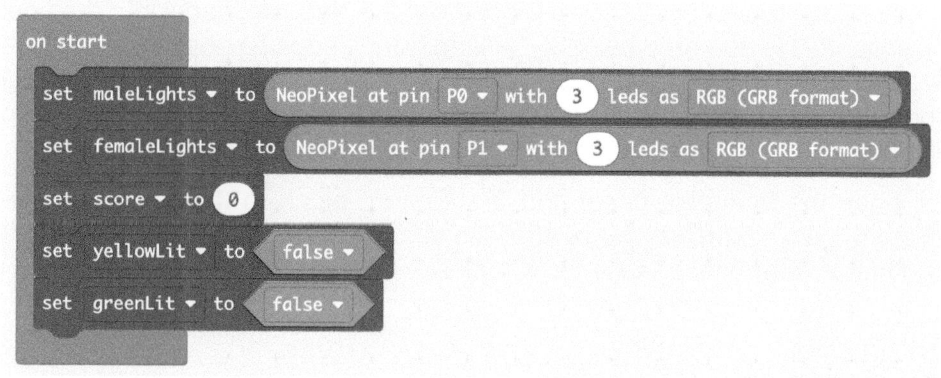

```
on start
  set maleLights ▾ to  NeoPixel at pin P0 ▾ with  3  leds as  RGB (GRB format) ▾
  set femaleLights ▾ to  NeoPixel at pin P1 ▾ with  3  leds as  RGB (GRB format) ▾
  set score ▾ to  0
  set yellowLit ▾ to  false ▾
  set greenLit ▾ to  false ▾
```

FIGURE 1.6: Starting elements in place

Step 3: Create the Male Firefly Flash Routine

Next, you can build the male firefly flashing pattern. Now, you need to use a loop to make something happen repeatedly.

> **Definition**
>
> A *loop* in the context of software is a control flow in programming that tells a computer to execute a set of instructions repeatedly, either until a condition is met or forever!

Open the Loops panel and drag the `every 500 ms` loop block to your workspace. Since male fireflies flash once every 10 seconds, change the `500` dropdown to `1000` since there are a thousand milliseconds in each second.

Now, you need to flash a yellow light on and off. You will set and reset the `yellowLit` variable to `true` and `false`, and you will add a pause in between the light flashes so they are easier to witness.

Drag the `strip show color red` block from the Neopixel panel into the new loop. Duplicate this new strip by right-clicking it and choosing duplicate. Change the two blocks so that the first becomes `maleLights show color yellow` and the second becomes `maleLights show color black`. From the Basic panel, drag a `pause 100 ms` block and clip it between the light flashes.

Finally, open the Variables panel and drag a `set` block to this area. Change your `yellowLit` variable to **true** after the light is lit and then to **false** after it turns to black. Your final panel should look like Figure 1.7.

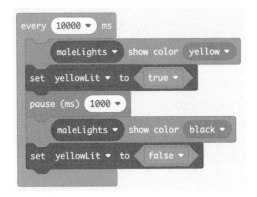

FIGURE 1.7: The final male panel

Step 4: Create the Female Firefly Flash Routine

Duplicate the block that you created for the male firefly LED flash pattern shown in Figure 1.7, but this time make the loop run using a random number between 1 and 10,000 milliseconds. Do this by dragging a purple `pick random` block from the Math panel and clipping it to the `every` loop block. Edit the two millisecond values to be 0 to 10000. Change the variables in the `set` blocks to reflect `femaleLights`. Edit the first `femaleLights` color drop-down to be green and the second one to be black (so you can see them better in the emulator). Change the `set` block to make the `greenLit` variable to be `true` before the pause and then `false` after the `femaleLights` turn black. Make sure that your blocks follow the order depicted in Figure 1.7 to complete the flash routine correctly. Your final female panel should look like Figure 1.8.

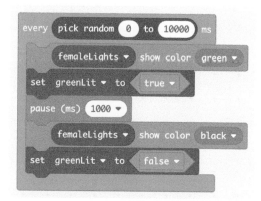

FIGURE 1.8: The final female panel

Step 5: Create a Condition for the Variables to Match and Get a Score

> **Definition**
>
> A *condition* in a software program helps you to make decisions by using statements such as `if...else...then`. You can compare items of similar types, such as strings to strings or numbers to numbers. The blocks you are using help you choose whether to use a string comparison or a number comparison. Strings are delineated with quotes (" "), and numbers default to 0.

The last thing you need to do is create a forever loop with a nested condition to check for matching variables, change the score if there's a match, and show the score in the micro:bit device.

From the Basic panel, drag a `forever` block that will run for the duration of your program into your workspace. This block will keep running forever or at least until something happens to make it stop.

In the Logic panel, find an `if` block and clip it into the `forever` block. This block will create a condition that will check whether both the yellow and green lights flash simultaneously, at which point you can consider that a match was made and the score increased by 1. Edit the `if` block to check whether `yellowLit` and `greenLit` are both `true`. Do this by finding a string comparison block from the Logic panel and clipping it into the `if` block, as shown in Figure 1.9.

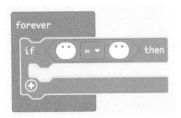

FIGURE 1.9: The conditional block

Add the variables you want to compare into the blank spaces of the block you just added. Drag a Boolean logic block to compare two values. Set the first values to compare to be the variables `yellowLit` and `greenLit` by dragging those two variables from the Variable panel into first small circle. Complete the comparison by dragging a Boolean block with the value `true` into the second circle, as shown in Figure 1.10.

Next, you need to make the score change by 1 and show it in the LED panel by manipulating the value of the score variable. To do this, add a variable block to change the score variable by 1 and clip it into the `if` block. You need to use the variable drop-down in the change block to choose the `score` variable. Finally, add a `show` block from the Basic panel to the end of the `if` block to display the score. Drag the `score` variable from the Variable panel and clip it to that `show` block. Now you have a full conditional that tests whether two lights are lit at the same time and changes and displays a score if so. The final blocks look like Figure 1.11.

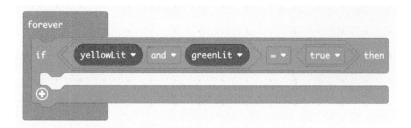

FIGURE 1.10: Testing two values

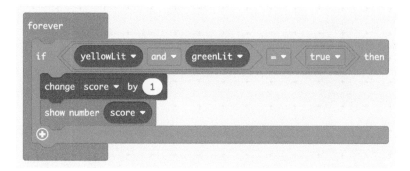

FIGURE 1.11: The final conditional blocks

When you run your final program, the four elements you built using blocks will start flashing, and when the flashes match, the score is incremented (increased by 1). Your final design looks something like Figure 1.12.

Congratulations, you built and emulated a firefly trapper that matches male and female flash patterns. Maybe you will be able to fool real fireflies and trap them using this system!

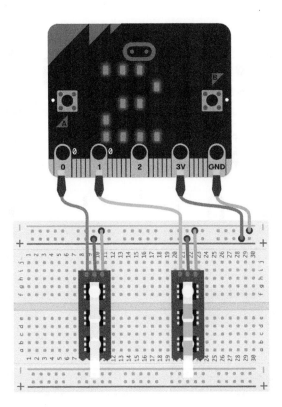

FIGURE 1.12: The final project

Extend Your Knowledge

Using a different light flashing pattern from your research, build a different Trapper that might succeed in luring fireflies of different species. Can you improve your "catch" score?

Vocabulary Review

In your own words, describe:

- Booleans
- Breadboard
- Hardware
- Sensor
- Server
- Software
- Variable

Quiz

Select the best answer for each of the following:

Q1: Micro:bit devices must be run on actual hardware.
    a. True
    b. False

Q2: The base color of the LED light on your micro:bit is
    a. Red
    b. Blue
    c. White

Q3: Conditions in blocks allow your code to
    a. Run faster
    b. Help you create lists
    c. Help you make decisions

Assignment: Let's Go Outside!

Using the downloadable worksheet at `https://cs4kids.club`, prototype a program for your micro:bit that can be used outside. An example would be to build a system that can be used to send you a message when someone comes to your door, or to light up when the sun goes down, or to make a garden gnome say something to unsuspecting passers-by who walk past your garden. A requirement of your system is that your hardware device should be able to connect to a website to enhance its functionality.

> **Note**
>
> You don't have to build this whole system, but draw a paper prototype of how the hardware and software might work together—for example, to log visits to your front door and store them in a database for display on a web dashboard.

Think of all the parts that need to work together in this system: hardware, software, cameras, and other sensors. Make note of how much it will cost to build the system, how it will be powered, and what it will look like, taking into consideration any protection needed by the hardware to keep it safe from damage.

2. The Firefly Refuge

Standard: 2-CS-01: Understand how to improve the design of a
computing device based on how it is used

You have built a firefly trapper prototype and are ready to demonstrate its capabilities to your Guide. While it simulates attracting and trapping the fireflies, however, you have only managed to catch one firefly in your hand. Perhaps it ventured near to you, drawn by curiosity, but now it seems frightened, beating its tiny wings against your hand and glowing fitfully.

The Guide walks toward you, and you can immediately sense disapproval and annoyance. Her glowing eyes flick toward you, and she snaps: "Why have you imprisoned my friend?" She pulls her cloak around her and stretches out her hand to the firefly. It flutters out of your hand and flies to her. She cradles it in her hand before releasing it into the night. As the firefly flies away, the Guide sighs. "Perhaps I didn't explain the outcome I'm looking for. We don't want to trap the fireflies into a prison, but rather we want to provide them with a home where they can find nourishment and rest." You willingly agree to the Guide's suggestions.

"Fireflies have been frightened away by intruders with bright lights such as the ones you just added to your machine. Light pollution can harm animals just as air or water pollution can! Convert your trap to an enclosed, darkened space and make it sense the light levels outside. Fireflies also like a warm environment, so you can add a temperature sensor to see if the temperature outside is appropriate for their comfort. If not, open the door to the house so that fireflies can enter the refuge and get away from the outside environment that does not meet their needs." It's time to convert your trap to a house!

Do Some Research

Do fireflies like cool, dark forests, or warmer environments? The report from the Singapore government's National Parks Service titled "Habitat Enhancements

23

for Fireflies," found at `www.nparks.gov.sg/-/media/cuge/ebook/citygreen/cg4/cg4_15.pdf`, has some good information about how fireflies prefer cool, damp environments with little ambient light. The article "Firefly Habitat," found at `www.firefly.org/firefly-habitat.html`, on the other hand, notes that fireflies prefer warmer environments (perhaps warm for North America is cool for Singapore). Finally, the `Nature.com` article at `www.nature.com/articles/s41598-021-91839-3` describes how light flash behaviors change in fireflies depending on their environment's temperature.

Based on these articles, you can set some baselines for the ideal temperature and best light level for the firefly population where you live and build a house for them as a refuge when their environment is not ideal.

Sketch It Out

Draw a quick sketch of the new design of your device. This time, it could be attached to a box with a servo, or motor, that can open and shut a door. It will need two sensors, one for temperature and the other for light levels, and these can be attached to the main micro:bit board. It might look like Figure 2.1.

Definition

A *servo*, or servomechanism, is a device that controls an element's physical position. Servos are often used when building a robot that has arms and legs that need to move or a mechanical arm that can open a door.

Your Challenge

Your job is to redesign your device without any dependence on LED lights, which are probably frightening away any potential firefly residents. This device must have the ability to open and close a door, so it needs a motor to be attached. If you don't have a micro:bit with a servo, that's fine! This project, like the previous one, can be completed entirely in the micro:bit emulator in a browser.

- Attach a servo with an arm that is able to open and close a hypothetical door.
- Attach a light level sensor to your micro:bit, and watch for temperature changes.
- Attach a temperature sensor to your micro:bit, and watch for light level changes.
- If the light level and temperature level are suboptimal for your firefly population, open the door using the servo and keep it open; otherwise, keep the door closed so that the fireflies can roam in nature.

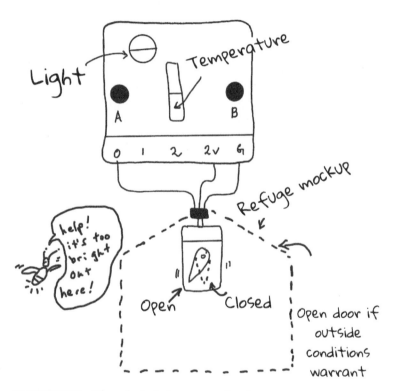

FIGURE 2.1: The sketch for your design

25

Project Recipe

In this project, you'll rethink your initial Trapper design. You'll turn it into more of a refuge to host fireflies.

Step 1: Create a New Project and Add a Servo Arm

On the micro:bit homepage (`https://makecode.microbit.org`) create a new project called **FireflyRefuge**. Click Extensions, which is listed above Advanced on the menu. Select **servo** to import the extension Servo—A micro-servo library. You should then see Servos listed as an option on your micro:bit menu.

Step 2: Build the *on start* Routine

Set up your variables. Drag a set variable strip into the `on start` block. As you did in Chapter 1, "The Trapper," create a new variable in the strip called `optimalLightLevel`. Drag a `false` block from the Logic panel and snap it to the variable strip. Duplicate that strip by right-clicking it with your mouse and selecting duplicate. Assign this new strip's variable the name `optimalTemp`, and make sure it's set to `false`.

> **Note**
>
> If you don't remember how to set up variables or what they are used for, refer to Chapter 1. You can manage variables using the Variables panel, where you can create them and assign them values, or you can create them directly in the blocks.

These variables will be changed in a timed loop if the light level and temperature become uncomfortable for the fireflies. Your `on start` block should look like Figure 2.2 after you've created your variables.

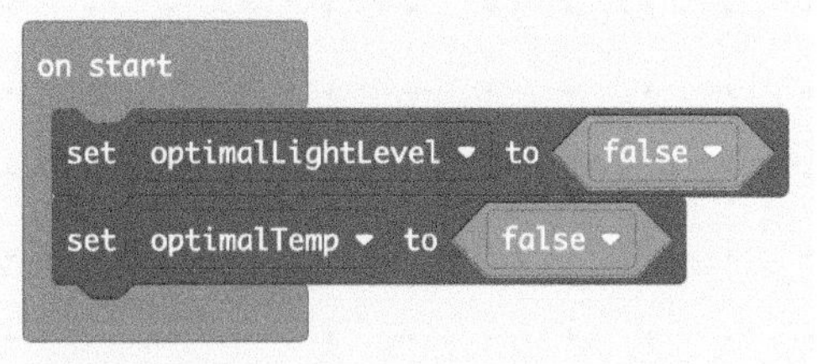

FIGURE 2.2: The on start block with variables added

Step 3: Add the Loop

Add a loop from the Loops panel on the menu to catch changes in temperature and light levels every 500 milliseconds. In the `every 500 ms` loop block, add three `if` statements (also known as conditionals) from the Logic panel by dragging an `if true then else` conditional block from the Logic panel into the loop. Duplicate this block twice so that there are a total of three conditionals. One of these blocks will test light levels, one will test temperature levels, and a third will check that both those levels are appropriate for firefly comfort.

In the first conditional statement, add a new conditional test to check the temperature level. To do this, drag an `and` Boolean logic block to your workspace and clip it into the conditional block to replace its built-in `and` logic. In the next two steps, you'll build a nested conditional to check for both a high and a low temperature level.

From the Logic panel, drag a numeric comparison block and clip it into the first comparison space in the conditional block you dragged in earlier. From the Input panel, drag a `temperature` (°C) variable and clip it into the first element of this numeric comparison block. Change the second element to **10** and change the comparison to **>**. This completes your first temperature check to see if the temperature is greater than 10 degrees Celsius. Repeat the previous steps to complete your comparison block, checking whether the temperature is also less than 34 degrees Celsius.

27

Now, build the rest of the conditional block. From the Variables panel, drag a `set` block into the body of the conditional statement and choose `optimalTemp` as its variable. From the Logic panel, drag a simple `true` Boolean into this set block to replace 0. Repeat this step in the `else` segment of your conditional, this time setting your Boolean value to `false`. Your logic is stating that if the first conditional check is `true`, then set `optimalTemp` to the Boolean `true`; otherwise, set `optimalTemp` to `false`.

Next, add a similar conditional check into the next `if` block to check whether the light level is less than 100 (or a level of your choice.) Light level is also a part of the Input panel. If the first conditional check is `true`, then set `optimalLightLevel` to the Boolean `true`; otherwise, set it to `false`.

Lastly, test whether the two variables are both `true`, and if so, keep the hypothetical door closed by setting the servo's angle to 90. Do this by dragging another Boolean `and` block into the last `if` block and clipping it to the `true` area. Build the logic of this section as you did for the temperature checks, this time checking that both the `optimalTemp` and `optimalLightLevel` variables are `true`. Complete the loop logic by dragging a positional servo block p0 from the Servos panel and setting it to **90** if `optimalTemp` and `optimalLightLevel` are both `true`. In the `else` statement, drag another positional block and set the servo's position to **45** to simulate opening a door. Now, your logic states that if the external optimal light level and temperature are appropriate for fireflies, the refuge is closed, but if not, the door is open for fireflies to seek shelter. Your loop blocks will look like Figure 2.3.

You probably noticed that, once you added temperature and light readings to your blocks, the micro:bit emulator automatically added some new elements to the device image, as you can see in Figure 2.4. You can test your logic by manipulating the thermometer image and light level image up and down with

28

your mouse. Test the validity of your program by changing light and temperature levels.

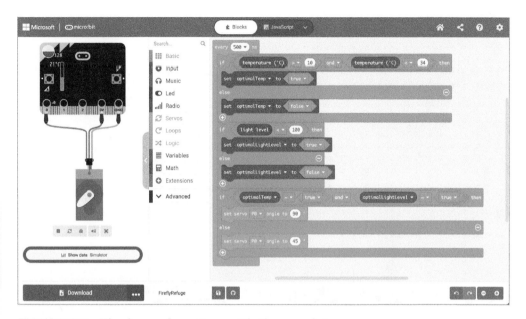

FIGURE 2.3: The looped routine with the emulator

Tip

If you get confused or are wondering how variables are being set, you can click the JavaScript panel to view your program as JavaScript. Add the line `console.log(yourVariable)` with the variable you want to check into the program. This line will appear in the block's code, and a console will appear in the workspace that you can check to verify that your program is working correctly.

Congratulations! You have created the basis of a system that could be connected to a box with a mechanical door that can open and close based on variables sensed in the environment. Manipulate the light and temperature sensors and watch the servo open and close.

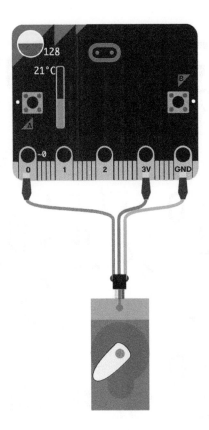

FIGURE 2.4: The device with everything in place

Think Like a Computer Scientist: Tailor Your System to Your Users

You've been given the task by the Guide to improve your device's design based on your observation of how users interact with it. This is an opportunity to think about the usability of your design. Think of how your device is designed to have two users: the Guide, who has asked for a device to solve a given problem, and the fireflies who have been attracted to it. While your device is a "firefly-computer interaction," the field human-computer interaction (HCI) is concerned with the interaction between regular users and computers.

Definition

Human-computer interaction (HCI) is the study of how people interact with computers with the goal of designing user interfaces that meet their needs.

Do a bit of research on HCI. How has it impacted the design of a particular device? Take a look at how various devices, like Apple iPhones and even older devices such as the telephone, have evolved over the years as they have been used by different people.

Extend Your Knowledge

Use a cardboard or wooden box with a servo attachment to build a residence for an animal or insect. You can create a sketch of a prototype if you don't have the parts handy. What kinds of animals or insects would benefit from a protective box? Think about its usability, both for the animal and for the human who might interact with it. Can you improve the design of a dog door so that it can be used only by a dog to enter and exit a house, while not allowing intruders?

Vocabulary Review

In your own words, describe:

- Conditional
- Operators
- HCI
- Servo

Quiz

Select the best answer for each of the following:

Q1: A servo is used to
   a. Control current
   b. Turn a switch on or off
   c. Open and close a door or latch

Q2: The Boolean data type can have one of two values:
   a. `true` or `false`
   b. `this` or `that`
   c. `if` or `and`

Q3: HCI focuses on
   a. Help desks
   b. Various types of sensors
   c. Interfaces between humans and computers

Assignment: Feed Me!

Your firefly shelter is able to sense light and temperature levels in an environment, but one thing it does not provide is nourishment, which was recommended by the Guide. Have you ever wanted to build a "smart" or "connected" feeder for your pet? Now's your chance! If you can, build a real device that can open and close a pet feeding device based on a button press or a motion sensor. If you don't have access to real devices, sketch a paper prototype of how you would build a pet feeder with a servo arm to open a door and dispense food.

> **Note**
>
> Here's something to think about: fireflies are carnivorous when they are larvae, because they feed on soft-bodied insects. When they mature, they feed on pollen. Some species of fireflies are very tricky—the females pretend to blink to attract males and then eat them! How would you create a specialty firefly-feeding device to address these scenarios?

Complete this assignment by building either a real device with a servo to feed a real-life pet and document it, a paper prototype of the ideal feeder (with its documentation), or a paper prototype of a specialized feeder for fireflies in various stages, also with a design document. Take into account the device's accessibility, ergonomics, and learnability and how easily your feeder can be accessed by its target audience.

3. The Fireflies' Message

Standard: 2-CS-03: Understand how to identify and fix issues with computing devices and components

You watch, fascinated, as dozens of fireflies stream into your new dark firefly refuge as long as you have your flashlight on. "They prefer the darkness, as do I," states the Guide, who closes the door of her lantern to create a darker environment. "Watch now, and perhaps they will send you a message."

Once inside their refuge, the fireflies glow merrily and land lightly on the floor of their new home. As you watch, you note that some fireflies land on buttons on each side of the refuge. Are they trying to tell you something?

"Can you enhance your system to allow the fireflies to communicate with you?" asks the Guide.

Maybe, if you could enable messages to be sent from the refuge by means of button presses or other taps, you could gather feedback from your guests, the users of your device. To send messages between devices, you will need a way for the devices to connect to each other, perhaps via Bluetooth, which is a radio connection, or by connecting the devices to the same Wi-Fi network. You can try a few things to get your refuge online.

By means of progressive experimenting, you can ensure that your device can communicate with a second device to gather feedback. You'll also need to perform troubleshooting tasks to make sure that the base refuge works even when its connected devices are offline. Ensuring that all the code runs without a glitch is called debugging, but in this case, your smoothly functioning refuge makes these lightning bugs very happy, and they blink on and off merrily.

Do Some Research

Devices such as the micro:bit can be connected to the Internet in various ways. They might be connected directly by wired connections, or they might connect over Wi-Fi. How, for example, does a device like a smart doorbell connect to the Internet? And how does it behave if some parts of the system it's connected to fail or are offline? Although someone pressing a button to alert you that they're at your door seems simple, there's a considerable amount of engineering behind the scenes. Let's consider it for a moment:

- First, the doorbell has to have some kind of power source, either wired (thus plugged into the home's power supply), a battery, or a solar panel of some kind.
- The doorbell has to be somewhat weatherproofed, even if it's on a sheltered porch, and should be able to withstand both high heat in the summer and freezing temperatures in winter.
- The doorbell probably has a button that, when pressed, sends a message to a connected user with a smartphone that there's someone at the door. Alternately, it might not rely on a button but rather on a motion sensor connected to a video camera so that you can see who's there without relying on a button. It might even have both a button and a motion sensor.

All these aspects of the doorbell have to be planned for and built as part of the device's systems architecture.

Systems architecture provides an outline of all the parts of a system and how the parts work together to create the whole. It includes both the hardware and the software elements and how they interact. It also includes a description of how a user interacts with the system and tests to verify that those use cases are well handled.

Consider all the parts of this system and how each one must be thoroughly tested so that if one fails, the other parts can handle that failure. Imagine you're the engineer of such a device. Think about the troubleshooting tasks you'd need to test and the problems you'd need to handle. Your list of tasks to test might look like the following:

- If the house power fails, send a message to the user via text and use a battery backup.
- If the external temperature rises above 120 degrees Fahrenheit, send a text describing the situation to the owner, shut down the system, and power it off to prevent heat malfunctions.
- If the button press fails to send a message to the homeowner, alert the visitor with an audio message to that effect and suggest knocking at the door instead.
- If the exterior is too dark to allow for an effective video feed, either switch to night mode or stop the video feed.
- Delete videos from the cloud after two years to save the cost of storage.

It's informative to do research on the decisions made in the real world when designing a system composed of many moving parts. By visiting the online troubleshooting help desk for products such as Google Nest (`https://support.google.com/googlenest`), you can get a good idea of all the scenarios that are tested and handled.

Think Like a Computer Scientist: Fix Problems

So many things can go wrong in even a simple computer system! Think about what happens when you turn on a computer. What needs to happen for all the various system components to start, or boot up, and for the computer to be able to run? What happens if the Internet connection is offline when you are trying to load a browser? What happens if systems are interrupted, such as when a code editor crashes before a file is saved? Software developers have to create a series of checks that can handle all the various failure points in a program.

In the case of your firefly messaging device, you can have a similar troubleshooting list of things that have to happen in case parts of the system fail. Such a list might look something like this:

- Connect to a wired power source. If there is no wired power source, send a message that the device is now using a battery. If the battery is dead, do not power up.
- Connect the base device to a series of other similar devices. In the next section you'll experiment with different ways of connecting to discover the best option.
- If other devices are online, allow users to send them messages—equivalent to "likes"—to express their opinion of the current refuge.
- Observe how many "likes" are expressed in a given refuge to be able to improve the other refuges.

While you won't be able to create this exact system in this emulator, you can see the "systems thinking" that needs to go into the architecture of these devices as they grow in scope and expand in functionality.

Sketch It Out

Sketch out the way you want your fireflies to send messages. While they could tap the logo to send a message or tilt the device one way or another, you can enable the A and B buttons to be pressed in order to express an opinion. You

38

can also prototype the way the devices connect to transmit these messages. Figure 3.1 shows a sample sketch of the way you could get the device to send a message on a button press to a connected device.

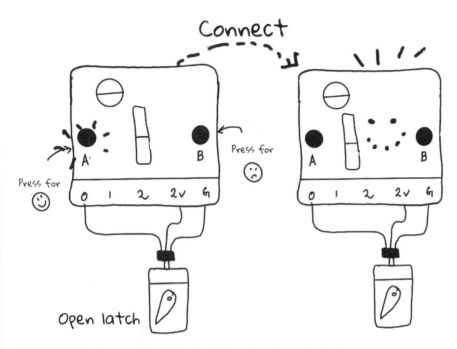

FIGURE 3.1: A sample sketch of the device with buttons

Your Challenge

You need to find a way for your device to send a message to a paired device, whether by connecting to Wi-Fi, radio, Bluetooth, or another protocol that will work with the devices you have available. Experiment to see what is possible with the devices you are using.

Debug your project if it doesn't properly connect. Try the following:

- Explore the various Wi-Fi integrations offered in the micro:bit extensions, now that you are familiar with using code from the community in your project.
- Try a Wi-Fi connector available in the emulator, such as the WiFi:bit extension. Are you able to make any of them work, given the limitations of your hardware at hand?
- Explore the debugging capabilities of the micro:bit emulator by importing a Wi-Fi module and attempting to connect it to your local computer.
- Find the best way to connect one device to another from this emulator, perhaps trying an HTTP request. Build a device connection so that one device can send a message to a connected device.

Project Recipe

To get started, duplicate the refuge project from Chapter 2, "The Firefly Refuge," calling it **FireflyMessenger**. You can duplicate a project by clicking My Projects ➤ View All and selecting a project to duplicate it. As you go, you can remove any extensions you don't use to keep your workspace clean. You can do so by going to the JavaScript console and then choosing the Explorer drop-down under the device image. Click the small trash can icon to the right of any unused extension to remove the extension from your project.

Note

If you try any of the extensions in your code, and then remove the extension before removing the extension's code from your project, your device image might not refresh properly. You might have to scan through the JavaScript code and manually remove the references to the missing extensions in your code. The device image should go back to being able to emulate your project.

Step 1: Set Up the Connection

In this step, you will do some experiments to find the best way for two refuge devices to connect to each other. Since this is an experiment, be prepared for failure! It's all part of the learning and prototyping process.

Note

As you progress with your projects, you'll discover that you often have to make a plan to build something, create what you think might be a solution, evaluate whether it works, and then make changes to the parts of your design that don't work well. This is all part of the design cycle described in the guide at `https://designstrategy.guide/ux/design-cycle-a-method-you-can-always-use`. You'll find that you iterate this cycle many times as you design a system.

Get started by going to the Extensions panel and searching for **WiFi**. Import the MakeCode extension for WiFi:bit. Drag an `on start` block to your workspace and, from the WiFi:bit panel, drag a `connect to WiFi network` block to the `on start` block. Input some network credentials that you may have handy. Ask the person who has control over the Wi-Fi network for credentials (maybe that's your parent or guardian).

Step 2: Create the Feedback Button

> **Note**
>
> In the images that follow, you'll find only the blocks relevant to this project depicted. Since you duplicated your project from Chapter 2, you'll have other blocks already built into your project to control the sensors and servos. Add more blocks as needed for this enhanced messenger project.

With your connection already created, from the Input panel, drag an `on button A pressed` block to the workspace. You're going to try to connect to a website from a Wi-Fi–connected device, so from the WiFi:bit panel, drag an `execute HTTP method` block to the button press block. Your blocks will look like Figure 3.2.

Try pressing button A in the emulator. What happens?

When you added the WiFi:bit extension, you might have noticed that a Show Data Simulator button became available under the device image. If you click that button, you'll discover debugging information about your Wi-Fi connection. Notice that, when you clicked button A in the emulator, the device tried to open a Google search using an HTTP method. Unfortunately, the operation fails, the returned message is `undefined`, and the connection closes (see Figure 3.3). This is because you can't use Wi-Fi connections in the micro:bit emulator. Too bad! You need to find a better way that allows the emulator to connect to another simulated device.

42

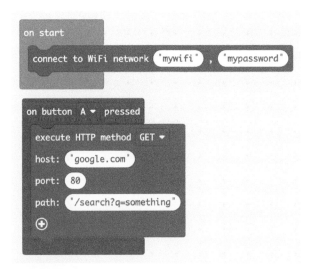

FIGURE 3.2: Trying to connect to Wi-Fi using the WiFi:bit extension

```
AT+CWJAP="mywifi","mypassword"
AT+CIPSTART="TCP","google.com",80
AT+CIPSEND=69
GET /search?q=something HTTP/1.1
Host: google.com
undefined
AT+CIPCLOSE
```

FIGURE 3.3: Errors connecting

Step 3: Create a Radio Connection and Button Actions

Let's try something different—a radio connection—to simulate paired connections between devices in the emulator. Start by removing the blocks from your current project or by starting a new project. From the radio panel, drag a `radio set group` block to the `on start` block. The `radio set group` block allows your device to belong to a gated group of micro:bits so that it will only send messages to a small group of connected devices.

43

Next, drag an `on button A pressed` block and an `on button B pressed` block to the workspace from the Input panel. Add a radio block to send a string `":)"` and `":("`, respectively. Your final blocks will look like Figure 3.4.

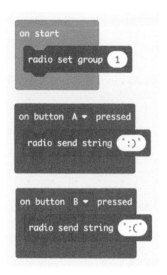

FIGURE 3.4: Connecting via radio

Note

This radio connection only works on the micro:bit emulator, as it simulates a direct connection between devices. The WiFi:bit connection, conversely, works only on devices that have a Wi-Fi attachment, since the micro:bit does not have Wi-Fi connection capability built in.

Step 4: Handle the Sent Strings

Next, you need to do something with the messages that were sent. You want to show the smile or frown image on a separate device when the correlating button is pressed.

From the radio panel, drag an `on radio received` block to your workspace to accept a string. This block ensures that any device belonging to radio group 1, which you just set in Step 3, will be able to receive a string. Add an `if-else` conditional block into that radio block from the Logic panel.

Drag a string comparison block from the Logic panel and clip it into the first element of the `if` block. Drag the `receivedString` variable name into the `if` block. You want to check if the received string is a smile, so type **:)** into the comparison area after the equal sign. If the string is a smile, you want a happy icon to show on the paired device, so drag a `show icon` block from the Basic panel and clip it into the first conditional result. Choose a "smiley" icon from the icon drop-down. Allow the icon to show for a few milliseconds, then clear the screen. To do this, add `pause` and `clear screen` blocks from the Basic panel to control the flow of the program.

If the received string is a frown, you want to show that icon in the paired device, so complete your conditional block by clipping an icon block from the Basic panel under `else`. Choose a frown icon from the icon drop-down. As you did with the smile icon, add pause and clear screen blocks to manage the message's appearance. Your completed blocks will look like Figure 3.5.

Now, your paired devices will reflect the messages sent by the fireflies. It's like Yelp for fireflies! Test your program by pressing the A and B buttons and watching the icons appear and disappear on the paired devices. The emulator now looks like Figure 3.6.

Extend Your Knowledge

Instead of using radio signals to connect devices, try a different architectural strategy (even if you don't have the actual parts needed to complete the project). Consider sending a text using a service like Zapier when the logo is tapped, or lighting up LEDs in various colors depending on the happiness of a refuge resident. How can you enhance this architecture to create a useful feedback loop? And what steps would you have to take to debug it and to ensure that errors are handled?

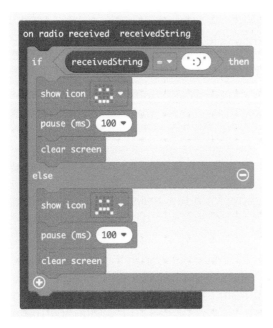

FIGURE 3.5: Receiving a string

Vocabulary Review

In your own words, describe:

- Debugging
- HTTP
- Software architecture
- Wi-Fi

FIGURE 3.6: Two devices connecting

Quiz

Select the best answer for each of the following:

Q1: Micro:bit devices need an extra layer of hardware to connect to Wi-Fi.
  a. True
  b. False

Q2: To send messages between only some devices, use:
  a. A wire
  b. A gated group
  c. An encoded signal

Q3: To discover and fix code problems and errors, use:
  a. A manual
  b. Debugging tools
  c. A radio signal

Assignment: How'd They Do This?

Think about a piece of connected hardware or software program that exists in your home or school and try to backward-engineer the thought process that went into its development. Examples include a smart thermostat, a connected refrigerator, or even a fictional Internet-connected toaster that you imagine might exist.

Construct a list to outline the development and testing processes needed to ensure that the device runs smoothly and that errors are handled. Start by describing what this program is designed to do, and then build a list or diagram showing the steps involved in the development process. Include the way that each step of the development process might have been tested to verify that it works.

4. A Home for All

Standard: 2-IC-21: Understand issues related to bias and accessibility in the design of existing technologies

As you watch the fireflies interact with your device, you notice that some do not use the buttons to send messages, but rather flutter fitfully around the devices or ignore the buttons entirely. "Why don't they send messages?" you wonder. "Are they unable to use the device, or are they uncomfortable?"

Your Guide shakes her head. "Remember, you initially set up the device to only be usable by one type of firefly, *Photinus brimleyi*. There are many, many other types that have their own needs, and unfortunately, your device isn't able to serve them."

This is a surprising and unwelcome bit of news. "I should have thought of attracting other types of fireflies from the beginning, I guess," you say, sadly. "It's a lot like all the other types of devices that are built today," notes the Guide. "A lot of them can only be used by a small set of people to do a limited number of things." You start to wonder about all the computers and smart devices out there. How usable are they for everyone?

Do Some Research

Accessibility is a hugely important topic in the field of computing. It's not just about the technology, but also about the people who use it.

Definition

Accessibility is the simple idea that devices should be usable by everyone, no matter their ability or disability. The field of accessibility focuses on creating and updating standards that ensure people with disabilities can use software and hardware devices, with or without using assistive technologies such as screen readers.

The software systems that are developed today must have accessibility baked in. In many cases, it's the law! You should research your country's laws about accessibility. In the United States, for example, you can find a list of accessibility laws online at `https://accessibility.gov`, and at `www.section508.gov`, you can learn about Section 508, the law that states that all websites must be accessible. Section 508 was added to the Rehabilitation Act of 1973 in 1998, so these laws have been around for many years. Familiarize yourself with this law and how it impacts the development of websites. Take a look as well at other laws either in the United States or in other countries that ensure that people with disabilities can access the web.

Think Like a Computer Scientist

Accessibility is best approached in the design phase of a project rather than after a project has been created. If you had started your firefly refuge project by deciding to serve many different types of fireflies, how would it function? What would the end-user experience be like? Put yourself in the role of a project manager of a team of software developers. It's your job to ensure that your project is accessible. Where would you address this task in your project plan, and what are the tasks that probably need to be done?

Some of those tasks involve rethinking how web pages should be built. Web and mobile programmers have many options when building accessible software. They should use tools such as semantic HTML, a color-safe palette, `alt` attributes for images, ARIA roles, and well-written links.

Let's break these down:

Semantic HTML   HTML is a way of creating web pages using tags or special words. Semantic HTML is a way of using the tags and special words such as `<header>`, `<footer>`, `<article>`, and `<author>` to help readers better understand the meaning of what is on a web page. Because these tags are descriptive, a screen reader can then more easily parse through a page, reading the tags out loud to help users with visual impairments.

Color-Safe Palette   Color-safe palettes are colors that make text readable for people with visual impairments by providing good contrast between background and text colors. These palettes also include colors that are distinguishable by people who have color-vision deficiency, also known as color blindness. If you are color blind, you might have trouble distinguishing between red and green colors, so your palette needs to account for this challenge.

In Figure 4.1, you can see how contrasting colors are much easier to see, even if your vision is perfect.

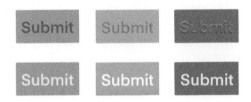

FIGURE 4.1: An example of contrasting colors for a submit button

alt Attribute   The `alt`, or alternate, attribute is a way to provide a text description of an image. This text can be read out loud by screen readers, so it's important to provide a description of the image. In addition, having good `alt` tags helps search engines discover your pages, so it's a win all around!

ARIA Roles   Assistive Rich Internet Applications (ARIA) roles are a way to provide a more descriptive role for elements so that they can be read by screen readers. For example, a link might be acting as a button, but if you want a screen reader to be aware that something will happen when you click it, you could add an ARIA role of `button`. In general, use semantic HTML tags like `<button>` for elements that act like buttons, but ARIA roles can come in handy on occasion.

Well-Written Links   A developer will probably need to create links when building a website, and they should be descriptive. A screen reader will read out loud the text of the link, so it's important to provide a description of what the link will do. If your link says "Click here," that's a lot less descriptive than having a link that says, "Visit our About Us page to learn more." Giving more information about what the link does means a screen reader will be more helpful.

> Note
>
> There are many tools to help evaluate your site's accessibility. Check the tool called Lighthouse against any web page and see what you discover! Lighthouse is available in your browser's developer tools. Right-click on any web page in your browser and select Inspect. In the developer tools, select the Lighthouse tab and use it to run a report on the accessibility of a website. Learn about Lighthouse at `https://developer.chrome.com/docs/lighthouse/overview`.

Sketch It Out

Sketch out a representation of a more accessible version of your devices that you have built so far. What changes could make them serve a larger population of fireflies? What about something as simple as allowing the fireflies to set their temperature preference by customizing the device to open the latch if the exterior light level is not to their liking? This would allow different types of fireflies to input their preferences and for the device to accommodate their needs.

In addition, fireflies may not be able to easily press buttons or use voice activation, but perhaps they can use the device's built-in ability to detect "tilt"—they can land on one side or another and tilt the device to set their light preferences.

Finally, displaying the preferred light preference setting will make it a more obvious choice for different kinds of fireflies. Figure 4.1 presents what your updated project might look like.

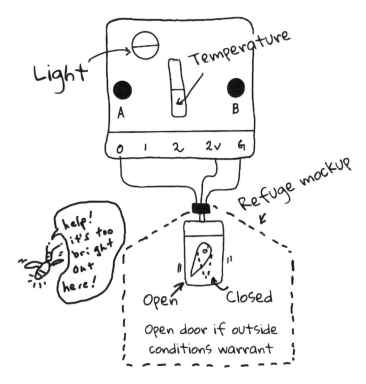

FIGURE 4.2: A sketch of a more accessible device

Your Challenge

In the sketch in Figure 4.2, a vision has been created to enhance the usability of one of your projects for your fireflies. Now you can build that vision into your emulator. You'll make a copy of your FireflyRefuge project and modify it to serve a larger population of fireflies by using the project recipe in the next section. If you have other ideas for other types of fireflies that you want to accommodate, feel free to alter the project to best serve your userbase!

In the following project recipe, you'll alter the firefly refuge to make it more suitable for different types of fireflies who have different requirements about the light levels that they prefer. Your task is to:

- Create a device that will respond to tilting right or left to set an optimal light level and display that number on the device.
- Build logic so that if the current light level is higher than the optimal light level, the latch to the refuge will open.

Project Recipe

Duplicate your FireflyRefuge project from Chapter 2, "The Firefly Refuge," as you did for your FireflyMessenger project in Chapter 3, "The Fireflies' Message," and delete all the code in the `every 500 ms` loop block. You'll build some new logic for this device but still make use of the servo arm.

Step 1: Set the Base Variables

From the Basic panel, drag a new `on start` block to your workspace. Create a new variable in the Variables panel called **optimalLightLevel**. Drag a `set variable` block from the Variables panel to the `on start` block and set this new `optimalLightLevel` variable to **100**. Drag another `set variable` block to `on start`, this time for `lightLevel`, and set it to **128**, the base light level set in the emulator by default. By setting these variables at the beginning of your program, you now are able to more easily reset and manage them as you move forward.

Step 2: Do an Initial Light Level Check

Next, drag a simple `if` conditional block from the Logic panel into your `on start` block. Here, you will check the light level and close the servo arm by default if the light level is greater than 0. This device responds to taps, so you can keep the latch closed to begin. Build this conditional block by dragging a number comparison block from the Logic panel and replacing the `true` Boolean placeholder in the comparison block.

54

Finally, drag a `set servo angle` block into the body of the comparison block and set its angle to 90 degrees. Your `on start` block looks like Figure 4.3.

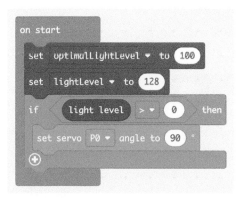

Step 3: Build a Tilt Mechanism

Next, you will want to leverage the device's ability to recognize that it's being tilted. From the Input panel, drag an `on shake` block to the workspace. Change its top drop-down to `on tilt left`. From the Variables panel, drag a `set` block into the `on tilt` block, and set the `optimalLightLevel` variable to **–10**. Do this by clipping an addition math block into the `set variable` block so that `optimalLightLevel` is set to `optimalLightLevel` –10. Next, you will ensure that the user can see what the value is of the new light level when there is a tilt. Drag `show number` blocks from the Basic panel into the `on tilt` block and set its value to **optimalLightLevel** so that this reading will be displayed on the device as it tilts.

Duplicate the `on tilt` block creation process to create an `on tilt right` block that will increase the `optimalLightLevel` variable by itself +10 when the device is tilted right. Your tilt blocks look like Figure 4.4.

55

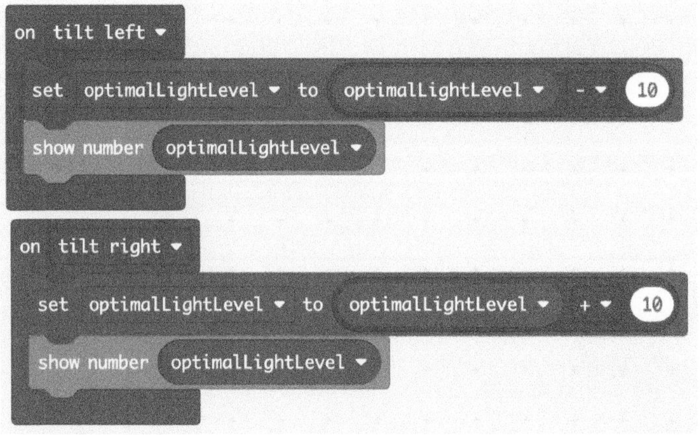

FIGURE 4.4: The `on tilt` blocks

Step 4: Complete the Loop

Now you're ready to complete the project by building a loop that runs every 500 milliseconds. This loop will be used to check whether the `optimalLightLevel` variable is less than the current light level, and if so, will open the latch to allow entry to a friendlier environment. Drag an `if/else` conditional block into this loop, and clip in a "less than" number comparison block at its top. Drag in the variables `optimalLightLevel` and `lightLevel` to the number values to be compared. In this way, the conditional check watches to see whether the optimal light is less than the current light. If that is true, then set the `set servo` block to be 45 degrees in an open position; otherwise, set the servo angle to 90. The final block looks like Figure 4.5.

Test your device by tapping on the left and the right side to watch it tilt in the emulator. See if the value of the optimal light level changes and the door can be made to open. When the device tilts, it looks similar to Figure 4.6.

Congratulations! You've built a much more user-friendly, accessible firefly refuge that really speaks to your audience's needs.

56

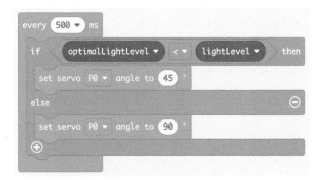

FIGURE 4.5: The final block

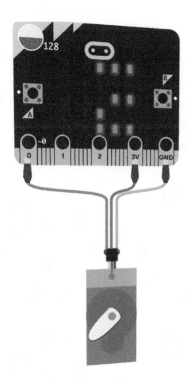

FIGURE 4.6: Your device

Extend Your Knowledge

You will find an interesting video demo on YouTube at `https://youtu.be/dEbl5jvLKGQ` that shows how a screen reader works. While you're there, explore videos of other ways that technology can be accessed by people who have different abilities.

Take a look at the special challenges of using mobile devices and how these devices handle challenges around accessibility. Think about how closed-captioning, audio descriptions, and other built-in accessibility settings found in smartphones are making these devices more usable. How do enhancements such as bold text, high-contrast color settings, the ability to make cursors more visible, dark mode, and settings to reduce motion help people who have visual impairments? Learn about Apple's Guided Access (`https://support.apple.com/en-us/HT202612`) and how it can help those with attention or sensory challenges stay focused. Then, compare iOS settings to Android (`www.lifewire.com/how-to-use-guided-access-android-4689158`).

Vocabulary Review

In your own words, describe:

- Accessibility
- `alt` attribute
- ARIA
- Lighthouse
- Screen reader
- Semantic HTML

Quiz

Select the best answer for each of the following:

Q1: Which one of these is an example of Semantic HTML?
   a. `<div>`

b. `<header>`

c. `<div role="button">`

Q2: ARIA stands for:

    a. Additive Rich Internet Applications

    b. Assistive Rich Internet Applications

    c. Assistive Ready Internet Applications

Q3: Accessibility encompasses:

    a. Color contrast, motion awareness, and readability

    b. `alt` tags, Semantic HTML, and well-written links

    c. Both a and b

Assignment: Usable or Not?

Pick a mobile app or website that you enjoy using and build an analysis of how usable it is, using the worksheet at `www.cs4kids.club/assets/ch4-worksheet.pdf`. If it's not accessible, how can you improve it? What could be enhanced to make it more accessible to other people? Then, dig deeper by considering the design thinking that went into the development of one part of the app or website. For example, if the app includes facial recognition or a fingerprint scan to log in, how do you think that technology was developed to ensure that everybody can log in? How was the design tested? How could it be improved?

II
The Glowing Moss

5. Goblin's Gold

Standard: 2-NI-04: Understand how to model rules around transmitting data

"Well done," says the Guide, as fireflies swirl around her happily. "You have solved the first challenge and are on your way to becoming a Forest Defender." Beckoning, she leads you deeper into the forest. A pale green glow wavers in the distance. "Come this way and see if you can help solve the mystery of the moss."

You make your way over a trickling brook and into a grove filled with protruding tree roots. Trying not to trip, you see an outcropping of boulders and underneath them, what seem to be patches of feebly glowing green light reflecting on a shallow pool. "This is *Schistostega pennata*, a very rare type of moss that can glow in the dark. Some people call it goblin's gold," says the Guide, bending down to observe it more closely. "It is able to glow because it is shaped like a lens and it can reflect light. But it seems so weak these days! Other types of mosses are choking it out because they grow better where there is sun."

"It's as if the forest network of trees, vines, grasses, and bushes are disrupting the transit of sunlight, causing the moss to weaken," you note. "Correct!" says the Guide. "Can you create a model of an optimal environment for this moss so that it can start to flourish here? In the process, you'll gain an understanding of how ecosystems are connected and how they share resources."

You turn to MakeCode's arcade to make a model to show the optimum placement of various mosses and plants to help them thrive. In the process, you learn about how data—in this case light—is transmitted, absorbed, and reflected by this moss.

Do Some Research

In this project, you will map out an ideal forest using MakeCode tilemaps, allowing a beam of light to reach an area of *Schistostega pennata* and its reflecting pool. While you're building your ideal map, keep in mind that this forest is not

63

the only type of ecosystem where data (in this case sunlight) is transmitted to support dependents. The Internet is something like this forest: data is transmitted using various protocols that govern the way data is carried from server to server, and eventually to an individual's Internet connection.

Think about how information, a signal, or a byte of data needs to travel from the cloud to your device.

Definition

A *byte* is a unit of data that is usually made up of 8 bits. Originally the byte encoded one single character of text on a computer. Bits can equal either 0 or 1. A combination of eight of these values can represent a character so that 01100001 represents the character *a*.

Your data has to get to its destination in the fastest possible way, following the best path. Sometimes, however, parts of a message can go missing. Computer systems have to be able to manage missing parts. Think of what needs to happen when some pixels of an image go missing. In what shape is the image eventually delivered to a device? Data might also need to have to be re-fetched from a server in case something happens during transit. And the device needs to be able to handle a request that never "resolves"—in other words, never reaches its destination.

The Internet is set up in a way that allows for data to be transmitted safely and securely, with fallbacks in case of error or dropped connections. Constructed as a network of layers, it relies on standard communication protocols, like a common language, that allows these layers to communicate with each other. Transmission Control Protocol/Internet Protocol (TCP/IP) is a common Internet protocol that has been around since the 1960s.

Now, imagine that the configuration of this network mirrors the challenge that your moss is facing. The various elements of the forest compete to be best positioned to get sunlight, just as they do in a real rainforest, and if they can't compete, they find other ways to survive in the forest canopy or on its floor.

If your moss is the recipient of data—in our context the ray of sunshine—what's the fastest way that it could receive the sunshine? What form should the sunshine take to be best received by the moss? If only a bit of sunshine is available, how should the moss react? Is there a good place for the moss to reside to better receive "clean" or unfiltered sunrays?

Think Like a Computer Scientist: Protocols

In Chapter 3, "The Fireflies' Message," we discussed protocols as a way of helping systems connect. Protocols are also a critical element in transmitting data across networks and the Internet. Think of protocols as rules that all computers follow when they send or receive data. These rules define the fastest path that data can be sent and received. They also define the way that data is handled when it is missing or corrupted. They handle special cases when data is sensitive or when it is not received in the correct order.

Think a bit about what a communications protocol actually does. As mentioned earlier, the goal of having a protocol is to ensure the clean transmission of data from server to client. A protocol includes a set of rules defining the format that the data must be in to be readable at its destination. A protocol includes, among other things:

- A format for data exchange
- A format for the sender and destination addresses
- A way to detect transmission errors
- An agreed-upon acknowledgment of successful data transmission
- A way to time out and retry a communication
- A way to control the flow of data, including which is sent first

To give a concrete example of a protocol in real life, consider what happens when you put a paper letter in a mailbox. You made sure to put it in an envelope with a stamp, a sender address, and a recipient address written on the front. Then, you placed it in a mailbox. At a given time, a mail carrier picked up the letter and took it to the local post office. Then a series of transmissions occurred to allow that letter to arrive at its destination by means of a network of post offices and mail carriers.

What happens if you forget to put on a stamp, if the paper is mangled in the post office, or if you misprinted the sender address? Your letter might be returned to you, marked "return to sender." This system is rather similar to how the Internet works, with a series of rules that govern transmission and errors of a packet of data, or a letter to your grandma.

Sketch It Out

You're going to create a game that mimics an element of a protocol as a bit of data (in our case, a ray of sunshine) making its way from sender to destination.

Sketch out a rough map of a forest similar to Figure 5.1. Represent the forest's elements as a maze for a ray of sunshine to navigate. Your forest might include various low-lying bushes that creep along the ground or climb up tree trunks like ivy. It might have vines that hang from larger trees. It might contain deciduous trees like oaks and maples that shed leaves each year, or evergreen conifers. Your forest might have tall grasses, shrubs, and other types of plants that are all trying to gather sunshine to survive.

Create a mini protocol made up of at least one rule. For example, if the ray collides with one of these elements, it causes loss of points or errors. You could also create a flow control so that your game loses points if a given transmission path or flow is not respected. You could also create an acknowledgment rule so that when the ray arrives at its destination, something interesting happens. Or you could create a timeout mechanism so that if your ray can't arrive at its destination within a given time period, an error occurs and the game stops.

Sketch out the types of forest residents that will populate a game that you'll make to map out a rule-based path from sun to moss. On paper, list the elements of a protocol that will ensure that the moss receives its light with at least one rule implemented. In the example that follows, the sunbeam loses "lives" if it collides with deciduous trees.

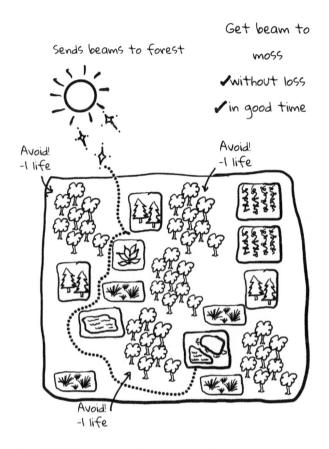

Sends beams to forest

Get beam to

moss

✓ without loss

✓ in good time

Avoid!
-1 life

Avoid!
-1 life

Avoid!
-1 life

FIGURE 5.1: A sample sketch of this maze game

Your Challenge

So far, your prototypes have used MakeCode for micro:bit, but now you can switch to the game-making tools offered by MakeCode, called the MakeCode Arcade, found at `https://arcade.makecode.com`. Your objective is to get the beam of sunlight to the moss as fast as you can, avoiding losing lives by colliding with deciduous trees.

In the following project, you're going to build a game modeling the transmission of a beam of light to a bed of moss. You'll do the following:

- Use tilemaps to draw various types of trees, shrubs, and grass. In MakeCode, tilemaps help you draw "walls" and you can detect collisions, as in a maze game. You'll also draw a special glowing moss tile that is the destination for the sunbeam.
- Create a movable sunbeam sprite. Sprites are a common element of 2D video games like those built in MakeCode's Arcade. Think of them as player characters.
- Build the game logic so that the sunbeam can interact with "walls" that prevent its passing through occupied parts of the forest.
- Arrange the forest as a maze with the object being arriving at the moss tile as quickly as possible, with the fewest losses of "life," within a time frame that is as short as possible, in order to get a good score.

Project Recipe

The following are instructions for how to make a tilemap to get a player (the sunbeam) to the destination (the moss) in a maze-like interface. Feel free to change the game logic and make it your own, and to either draw the game elements yourself in MakeCode or use existing ones available in the interface. It's very fun to draw your own custom elements, so we'll walk through how to do that next.

Step 1: The Arcade

Open the MakeCode Arcade at `https://arcade.makecode.com`. This is a designer for retro-style pixel-based games that you build yourself using blocks, JavaScript, or Python code. MakeCode Arcade works just like the micro:bit interface you've been using in previous chapters but uses a game-like emulator instead of a micro:bit emulator. It also includes a few different items in the menu that help with building games, giving you the ability to control *sprites*, which are movable elements; add music and sounds; build scenes; manage scores; and more. To test your game, you can click the triangle play button to see your progress.

Step 2: Build the *on start* Block

In an `on start` block, start designing your interface. From the Scene panel, drag the `set background color to` block to your `on start` block and choose a forest-looking color.

Step 3: Build the Tilemap

Open the Assets panel at the top of the screen and use the plus sign button to create a tilemap. Use the tilemap to build a map in the form of a maze. In the

Tilemap panel on the left side of the tilemap builder, select the My Tiles tab, click the plus sign to create a new tile, and then use the pencil and various colors to draw a custom tile for your maze. If you make a mistake, use the erase button next to the pencil. Click Done when you have completed a tile. The custom tile will be added to your custom tile panel. Remember, you're creating a forest scene, so your tiles can be a tree, such as in Figure 5.2, or some grasses such as in Figure 5.3, or other things that might grow in your forest.

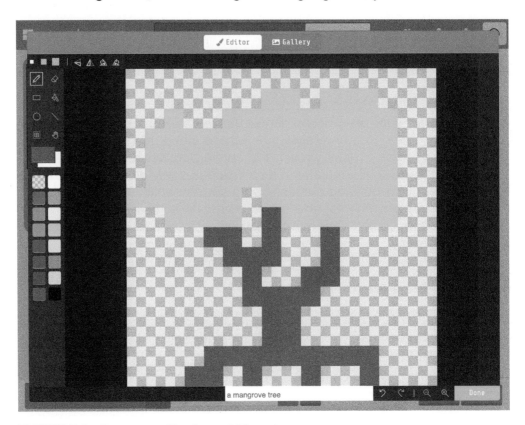

FIGURE 5.2: A custom tile shaped like a tree

Source: Microsoft Corporation.

When you're done creating your custom tiles, click Done in the custom tile panel. Then, add the tiles to the tilemap in clusters by selecting a custom tile from the left panel and dragging your mouse across the tilemap area. In the example shown in Figure 5.4, there are groups of tall grasses, deciduous trees, vines, and conifers.

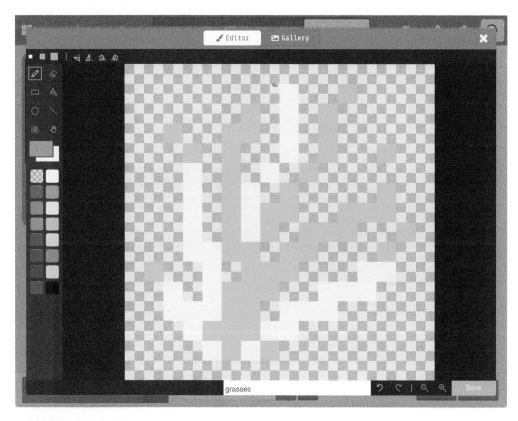

FIGURE 5.3: A custom tile shaped like grasses

Source: Microsoft Corporation.

Create one tile to represent the moss and place it in a corner of your tilemap. It can look like some glowing green squares, or you can make it hidden inside a cave structure and have a pond in front of it, as we did. Your tilemap might resemble Figure 5.4.

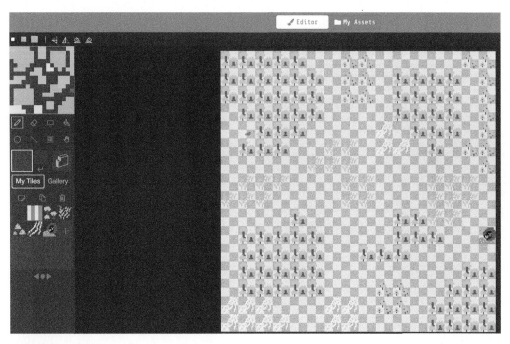

FIGURE 5.4: A tilemap for your game

Source: Microsoft Corporation.

Step 4: Build the Walls

Now you're going to build walls that overlie your tilemap but aren't seen by the player. They function to block access to various areas on your map. You can cause players to lose points by bumping into a wall.

Build the walls of your tilemap by using the wall tool in the tilemap building tool (in Figure 5.5, it's the highlighted icon above the Gallery tab). Click the wall tool so that it is highlighted in red and drag your mouse over the areas of your tilemap that you don't want to be passable by a player. They will look like translucent red squares, as in Figure 5.5. Build the walls so that they do not cover the entire group of each forest element; that way, you can stop the player from crossing that area. The walls might resemble Figure 5.5. Click the Done button when complete.

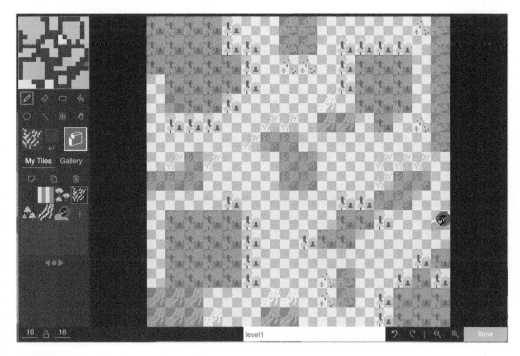

FIGURE 5.5: A tilemap's walls

Source: Microsoft Corporation.

Open the Scene panel and drag the `set tilemap to` block into `on start`. Select the tilemap you just created in this block's drop-down. Now your game has a maze!

Step 5: Add Sprites

When your tilemap is complete, you're ready to add a sprite to the maze to navigate through it. Returning to the blocks workspace, open the Sprites panel and add a `set my sprite to sprite of kind...` block to your `on start` block as type Player.

Click the gray box in the `sprite` element in that block to customize it. In the window that opens, you can design your sprite to resemble a sunbeam by drawing a sunny, star-like shape. Click Done when finished.

Rename this sprite beam by creating a new variable in the block's drop-down.

You also need to set the starting position for your sunbeam sprite so that it starts the game in a logical position. From the Sprites panel, drag in the `set Sprite to position x 0 y 0` block and change its drop-down to **beam**.

Click the position numbers in the block and set the player to start the game in a place that does not overlap any forest element. For the demo game, we used 98 for x and 3 for y, which means 98 pixels from the top-left edge and 3 pixels down from the top edge. Customize your settings to suit your tilemap layout.

> **Note**
>
> When you are working with the pixel value, a pop-up appears to help you set the right position for your sprite.

Step 6: Set the Camera

Next you need to create a camera in your game that will be able to follow your sprite's progress as it moves through the maze.

Scroll down in the Scene panel to Camera and drag the block `camera follow sprite mySprite` to the `on start` block. Use the drop-down to change the camera to follow the sprite called beam so that as the player walks through the maze, the camera follows it.

Step 7: Set the Beam's Position

Next, you need to provide instructions for the controller, which is the little joystick element in the game emulator, to make the sprite move around. In the Controller panel, drag `move mySprite with buttons +` to the `on start` block. Edit the block's drop-down to refer to `beam`.

Edit this block by clicking the plus sign so that `vx 100 vy 100` appears. These settings control the velocity of the beam as it speeds through the maze. You can edit these numbers to speed up or slow down the beam's speed.

Now you can test your game so far. You should be able to click the joystick to make your sunbeam move around the game, and it should stop where you have placed walls above your tilemap. Give it a try!

Step 8: Fine-Tuning

Finally, from the Info panel, drag the `set life to 3` and `set score to 0` blocks into the `on start` block. Edit these defaults to your liking—they will change as the game progresses. In Figure 5.6, you can see that the value for life is set to 100 and that the score is also set to 100. You can make the game more or less difficult by setting the life to a lower or higher number. Experiment with the numbers to see what is realistic based on the game dynamics. Your completed `on start` group should look similar to Figure 5.6.

Step 9: Add a Timer

Now, you can start enhancing the way the game is played so that you can actually win it by getting the beam to the moss within a given time. Add a timer that will display in the right-hand corner and will decrease the score each second that the game runs. Drag the `on game update every 500 ms` block from the Game panel to your workspace to do this. Edit this block's drop-down to change to **1 second** so that the timer will fire every second. In this block, drag `change score by 1` from the Info panel, editing it to decrease the score by

–1 every second of the game. You can customize this block to your liking, but in general this countdown can show a loss of points as the game runs.

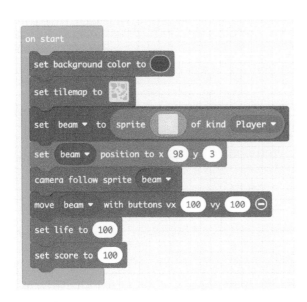

FIGURE 5.6: The on start block

Source: Microsoft Corporation.

Also in this update block, add a consequence for running out of time: from the Logic panel, drag a simple `if true` conditional block into the `on game update` block. Drag a numeric comparison block from the Logic panel and clip it into the conditional area to replace `true`. From the Info panel, drag the `score` variable and replace the first 0 in the comparison. Finally, drag a `game over` block from the Game panel and set a losing condition. You can add a cool effect by clicking the plus sign in the block and adding a visual effect (we chose the cloud effect). Now, your game can update every second to decrease the score by 1, causing the player to lose after 100 seconds of play. Better be quick to get through this maze!

In general, you want to make a game that encourages users to move through the maze as quickly as possible without losing too many lives, as in Figure 5.7.

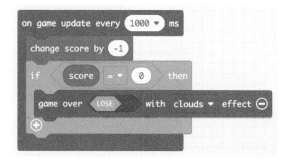

FIGURE 5.7: A scoring timer

Source: Microsoft Corporation.

Step 10: Build Collision Logic

Now, build the collisions. A life will be deducted from the player for each collision with a wall. Open the Scene panel and add an `on sprite of kind Player overlaps at location` block to the workspace. This block is found under the Tilemaps section of the Scene panel. Remember how you built walls over your tilemap images? These items are the basis for this collision logic. Add a number of these blocks corresponding to how many types of forest elements you created while drawing the tilemap. In this demo game, we decided, according to the protocol that we mapped out at the beginning, that only colliding with deciduous trees would cause loss of life, so therefore we will need only one of the blocks mentioned earlier. Edit this block to refer to the deciduous tree tile (or whichever element you want to avoid) by selecting the image of that tile in the drop-down. Repeat this procedure if there are other tiles where you want to track collisions.

From the Info panel, drag `change life by -1` to each of these blocks. Duplicate the `game over` block with its conditional from the timer block, changing `score` to `life`, which you'll find in the Info panel. The resulting block should look like Figure 5.8, but you can make your game more challenging by setting different tile collisions to have different behaviors, as you defined them in your initial protocol plan.

77

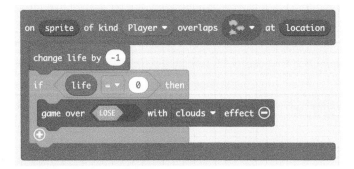

FIGURE 5.8: Calculating lives

Source: Microsoft Corporation.

Step 11: Build the End State

Lastly, build the end state of the game by adding one more overlap block to the workspace, choosing your moss tile from the tilemap. From the Game panel, drag a `game over` block and choose WIN when the player overlaps the moss. You can experiment with adding an effect by clicking the + button in the `game over` block and then using the drop-down to show confetti, sparks, stars, or bubbles, as you prefer, as shown in Figure 5.9.

FIGURE 5.9: Game over!

Source: Microsoft Corporation.

Step 12: Test Your Game

Test your game a few times. Is it too difficult or too easy? Make tweaks to your game logic until you like it. Make sure that you have implemented a protocol

78

that will ensure that the moss receives its light in an optimal way. Your final game might resemble what is shown in Figure 5.10.

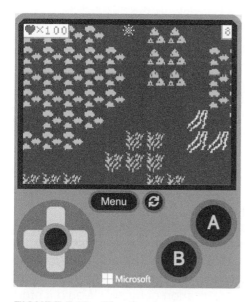

FIGURE 5.10: The final scene

Source: Microsoft Corporation.

These instructions will allow you to build a basic maze game with game logic resembling the protocol for getting a piece of data from point A to point B while handling "loss." You can enhance it quite a bit to create different challenges, sounds, ways to win and lose, and more, following your plan as you outlined earlier.

Extend Your Knowledge

Now that you are thinking about how to get a signal quickly from start to finish without loss of power, you can apply your understanding to thinking about how this translates to the Internet. Explore the various types of protocols that govern the Internet such as TCP/IP. Try to envision one of these protocols in the context of your forest. How would you configure the best designed forest environment to resemble a well-architected information network? Would it start to resemble a formal garden or remain a wilderness?

Vocabulary Review

In your own words, describe:

- Byte
- Protocol
- TCP/IP
- Tilemap

Quiz

Select the best answer for each of the following:

Q1: A tilemap is used to create:
- a. A wall
- b. A hedge
- c. Both of these

Q2: The Internet is set up in a way to allow fallbacks in case of error or dropped connections.
- a. True
- b. False

Q3: TCP/IP is:
- a. A kind of server
- b. A kind of website
- c. A set of communication protocols

Assignment: Draw the Map

In this chapter, you learned about protocols and how they help the process of transmitting data across networks and the Internet. Protocols define how messages are transmitted, something like how you defined the best path for your sunbeam to travel to arrive at the moss. Now it's time to apply your knowledge to the real world. Imagine that a message, stored in some server in the cloud, has to travel from that server to your inbox.

Draw a map of the best secure path for that message to take to arrive in your inbox intact. Note that the message could be a large batch of text, an image, or a video. The message could also be coming from a server, and you want to receive it on your phone. Draw a map of a network to visualize your message's route. Don't forget to note the ways that messages can be corrupted or lost.

6. Securing the Moss

Standard: 2-NI-05: Understand how electronic information can be
protected using physical and digital security measures

Looking closely at the tiny moss colony, you see that it grows best in areas
protected by the largest tree roots, shaded by the thickest branches, under rock
outcroppings, or even in deep in caves with little light. In other areas of the grove,
you see that different types of moss have grown where there is more light. You
notice that intruding moss tends to compete with the fragile luminous mosses,
which rely on light sources in subtle ways, such as a beam of light reflected in a
pool of water. Moreover, you notice footprints around the moss itself and empty
patches where moss has been removed.

Someone has been trying to collect the luminous moss, probably to add to a fancy
terrarium! "You see?" says your Guide. "We need to discover a way to protect this
rare species from theft and environmental degradation. Is there a way to build a
barrier, perhaps with a lock that can be opened with a password, that will still let in
the light but stop intruders from taking the moss?"

Working with your map, you create a porous barrier with a secure lock that can
be opened only by someone with a password. The barrier creates a dome over
the moss, allowing light through, but is physically impregnable to anyone without
the password. In this way, you prototype for the Guide a way to better protect the
patch of moss from intruders, improving its physical security while protecting its
light-collection ability.

Do Some Research

How have people traditionally secured their precious objects? Do some
research about physical and nonphysical patterns of security. Banks, for example, might have a physical barrier that protects their vaults from thieves. But
there are many more layers of security, almost like peeling an onion. Imagine,

for example, the security that you must go through to access a bank teller and make a withdrawal in person. First, you might use your bank card to open the front door, then again use your bank card or write a check to withdraw money from your account. You might use an automated ATM, in which case you use a different process to access money from the machine.

How has software mimicked and surpassed these patterns of physical security? Explore W3 School's Cyber Security chart found at `www.w3schools.com/cybersecurity/index.php` to learn more about the different types of security. Pick a topic and explore it in depth.

Think Like a Computer Scientist: Barriers

Whenever information is made available online, it can potentially be accessed by anyone. For this reason, it is important to protect your information from unauthorized access. The best way to do this is to use secure barriers, using physical means such as locked server rooms as well as digital means such as firewalls and password protection. Think about all the various barriers that protect information. And there is probably cybersecurity, security that protects data as it moves around on the Internet and is stored in various places online.

Sophisticated techniques have been developed to protect valuable data assets. While they are all various types of barriers It's useful to gain a good understanding of the various protections that have been designed, whether physical or digital:

Disaster Recovery   When catastrophic events occur, from power outages to cyberattacks or civil unrest, there should already be plans in place to prevent data loss and loss of business. Lists are made of the most vulnerable systems and steps are taken to ensure that they have a way to "fail over," or move from a failed device to a backup device. A plan is prepared so that, if disaster strikes, there is minimal disruption.

Firewalls   Firewalls are a common software system that monitors traffic on a network, allowing some and blocking others based on defined security rules.

Interestingly, this software was named after a physical barrier against fire. Firewalls protect networks from risky data transactions.

Secure Storage   When files need to be stored securely and backups preserved, systems can be put into place to ensure that data is not lost if a storage unit fails. Passwords and user credentials need to be stored securely as well, in a form that can't be easily read by anyone, including the database administrator. Various encryption strategies are available to protect passwords, but if the password itself is easy to guess, computer programs can crack them more or less easily. For this reason, it's important for web applications to require a user to have a well formatted, secure password and for databases to store them with proper encryption.

Secure Protocols   In the previous chapter, we learned that protocols are rules guiding the best way to transfer data over networks. The use of secure protocols such as Secure Hypertext Transfer Protocol (HTTPS) ensures that data traveling over the Internet from input areas such as forms and logins remains secure and encrypted.

While no one barrier or security protocol is foolproof, when combined they can form a secure system that helps provide a level of security appropriate for the needs of your applications.

Your Challenge

You need to prototype a security mechanism to ensure the survival of the luminous moss in the face of encroachment by building a more protective environment. Build a barrier that is strong, yet porous enough to let light in, and that is impregnable to intruders who do not have a password.

Sketch It Out

You have to create both a physical barrier and a way to open the barrier with a password. Sketch out the flow that will allow a person to open the barrier with a password. Your sketch might resemble Figure 6.1.

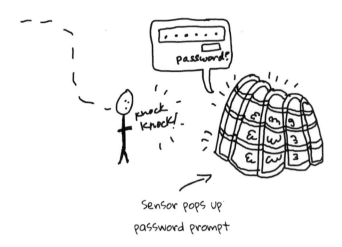

Sensor pops up password prompt

FIGURE 6.1: A sample sketch of the barrier

Project Recipe

Create a new project in MakeCode Arcade and name it **SecureMoss**. This will not be a full, playable game, but rather a prototype of how your security around the moss can be set up. You need:

- A sprite for your moss
- A sprite that is a barrier to protect your moss
- A pop-up that will appear when button B is clicked to lift the barrier for access if a proper password is entered

Step 1: Create Your Sprites

Start by working in the game editor with the new game that you created. You'll need two sprites, `door` of kind `barrier` and `moss` of kind `Player`.

Create the moss sprite by dragging a `set mySprite to sprite of kind Player` block from the Sprites panel to the `on start` block. Rename it **moss** by using the first drop-down in the block. Click the gray square in that block to design a glowing, moss-like sprite. Maybe your sprite can be green with yellow sparkles.

Now you need to create a door sprite. This sprite will have a new kind, `barrier`, that will be used to protect your moss. Duplicate the moss block that you created earlier, calling this new sprite **door**.

In the second sprite block, draw a green bamboo door or gate in a lattice pattern to change its appearance, similar to what is shown in Figure 6.2. In the block's kind drop-down, create a new kind of sprite, **barrier**, and select that as the door's type.

FIGURE 6.2: Glowing, sparkling moss

Set the moss to have a cool radial effect, as shown in Figure 6.3, by dragging a `mySprite start spray effect` item from the Sprites panel. Choose moss in the drop-down and a cool radial effect, which causes a sort of sparkly spray to emanate from the sprite. You can also pick some other effect that you like to make the moss glow.

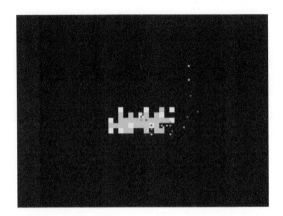

FIGURE 6.3: Moss with a radial effect

You might have noticed that the door and moss sprites seem small in the emulator. Make your sprites interact more realistically by making the barrier appear larger than the moss so that it encircles and protects it. To do this, you might need to edit the sprites' sizes. Feel free to edit the sizes to suit your needs.

- To make the gate larger than the moss, resize it by setting the door to scale by 5 and anchor it in the middle. Do this by dragging the `set mySprite scale 1 anchor middle` block from the Sprites panel (scroll to the bottom) to the `on start` block and changing `mySprite` to `door` and its scale to **5**.
- Similarly, set the moss to scale by 2 and also anchored in the middle. Duplicate the block you added to scale the moss's size and add it to the `on start` block, changing its drop-down to `door`. Change the scale and effects associated with your sprites according to your vision of the door and moss.

Step 2: Create the Password

Next, create a password that will be used to protect the moss from access. Only people with the correct code will be able to enter. Drag a `set` block from the Variables panel to the `on start` block and use the drop-down to create a new variable called `code`. Then give that variable a value, which will be your password. The value of your code variable might be **222**. Once you've added the sprites and variable, your `on start` block should resemble Figure 6.4.

> **Note**
>
> Research the best practices for storing passwords for use by customers, clients, or players. What you just did by creating a variable and assigning a specific value would be called *hard-coding* the password into a program. Not only is the code that you created very short and repetitive, but it's also easy to guess and anyone could discover it just by looking at the code-base. Clearly that is not a best practice.

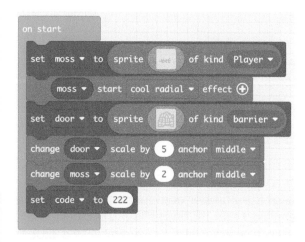

FIGURE 6.4: The `on start` routine

Source: Microsoft Corporation.

Step 3: Program the Barrier

Now you need to force the user to enter a password to lift the barrier. You are going to use the B button in the emulator to simulate approaching the barrier and attempting to gain entrance to look at the moss (but not to touch it!). You will be prompted with a pop-up to enter a password. If you successfully enter a password that matches what you set earlier, the barrier will open and you will be able to see the moss.

From the Controller panel, drag an `on A button pressed` block to the workspace and use its drop-down to change it to the **B** button. In the following substeps, you'll build what happens when that button is clicked.

Note

In the MakeCode emulator, the A button is used for entering the digits into a form, so you'll use the B button to simulate the approach.

Substep 1: Add a Conditional

First, add an `if/else` conditional block to the on `B button pressed` block. You're going to build some logic to check whether the user enters the proper password.

Substep 2: Limit the Input Field's Length

Edit the `if` conditional by clipping a number comparison from the Logic panel to replace `true` in the block. From the Game panel, drag an `ask for number` block and clip it into the first space of the number comparison. Edit that `ask` block by clicking the + button and ensuring that the length is **3**. This logic is like a web form that checks that someone has entered a password of the proper length. You've probably used similar web forms to check your email or sign up for a service online.

90

Substep 3: Compare the User's Input to the Password Value

Complete the comparison by changing the block's drop-down to **is not equal** and drag the code variable from the Variables panel, clipping into the final element of this comparison. This edit to the `if` statement checks whether the user entered something invalid, either an empty password, something of the wrong length, or something that does not equal the variable `code`.

Substep 4: Add a Helpful Error Message

Complete this conditional check by dragging a `show long text` block from the Game panel and adding it to the initial `if` conditional. Edit it so that the error message appears as **wrong password!** and change the drop-down to **full screen**. That's an error message that can't be missed!

Substep 5: Test Your Program

Test your program so far by clicking the B button, which simulates someone approaching the gated moss. A pop-up prompt should appear, with a request to enter a password. Use the joystick to navigate the buttons, navigating to click OK with the A button to enter the code. If it's the wrong code, the error pop-up should open; you can close it by pressing A again. The password box looks like Figure 6.5.

FIGURE 6.5: The password box

Source: Microsoft Corporation.

91

Now, complete the `else` element, which will be shown when the password is correct. You can have some fun by creating an animation to open the gate, since the user will have entered the proper password.

Note

Research the best way to allow users to enter their passwords and send them over the Internet. Normally, sending passwords in clear text is a bad idea. In general, passwords are sent from a web form to a server for authentication. But is your password just sent right over in clear text? How is this data protected? In a properly architected form, the password is sent over a connection protected by HTTP with a secure layer provided by an SSL certificate (a secure socket layer). This provides a secure "tunnel" for credentials to pass through forms that should be using Authentication headers in their code to send usernames and passwords. Always check a browser's URL in a website to see if it is using SSL—you can tell by the use of `https` in the address bar and a small lock icon that shows the site is secure.

Step 4: Opening the Barrier

If the password is correct, an animation will appear to open the door. You can create an animation by opening the Advanced ➢ Animation panel and dragging an `animate mySprite frames` block to the `else` area of the conditional. Choose door in the drop-down to build the behavior of the door sprite. Next, you will draw the frames of your animation to make the door seem to open.

To create an animation, click the gray box, which will open the Assets panel. Think for a minute how you want the animation to look. If you envision a gradual lifting of the door, go to the Assets tab and create a new animation by using the + button. Create a copy of your green gate by selecting it in the Assets panel and clicking copy. Open the new animation you created earlier by selecting it

92

in the Assets panel and clicking edit. Paste the copied gate image into the first frame of the animation by pressing Ctrl+V on your keyboard.

Now you're ready to animate the door. From Assets, open your new animation. On the right side of the Animation Editor, you can create frames. Start with four frames. Paste the door image into each frame. Use the marquee tool on the left side of the Animation Editor to select the door image and move it up gradually until it disappears in the last frame, to create an illusion that the door is lifting from the moss. Your animation frames might look like Figure 6.6.

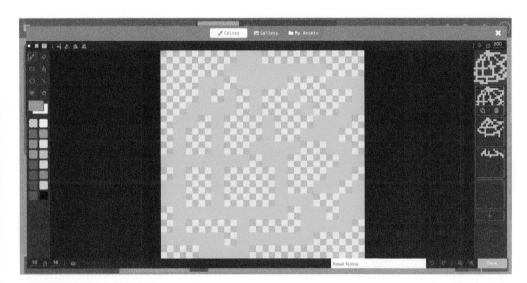

FIGURE 6.6: Animating the barrier
Source: Microsoft Corporation.

Be as simple or as detailed as you like in your animation. When you're done, make sure that animation is selected in the Animate panel in the `else` part of the conditional block. Change the interval to your liking, and make sure the animation does not loop or repeat itself. To test the animation, you can drag it temporarily to the `on start` block to see it in action before putting it back into its place.

93

Once the animation is complete, the moss will be fully visible to the player. Test your secured moss system's password entry and animation by entering the correct password to gain access to the moss. Your block code looks similar to Figure 6.7.

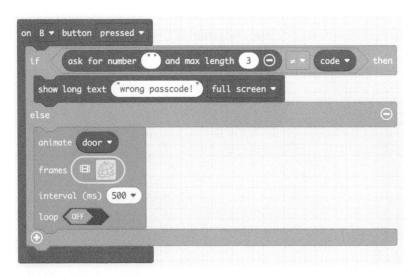

FIGURE 6.7: The B button clicked

Source: Microsoft Corporation.

Extend Your Knowledge

In your prototype, you hard-code, or write in code, the password that users will have to use. In real applications, users usually set their own passwords to gain access to a system, or a central authority issues a password and keeps it secure. Research the ways that passwords are used in real life and how they can be used in your prototype. Study the patterns used to enable users to set, reset, and verify their passwords. To do this, they need to verify their identity, so study ways in which apps and mobile devices verify identity using techniques such as face identification or fingerprints. Can you think of ways that these systems can be cracked or compromised? What is the most secure system that you can visualize? Is it usable?

An interesting code challenge would be to create a micro:bit integration that would function as a "locking" device. It could detect movement in the area using a sensor, and immediately pop up a window asking for a password. A useful tool for diaries and other items you want to keep from prying eyes!

Vocabulary Review

In your own words, describe:

- Animation
- Disaster recovery
- Passwords
- Security

Quiz

Select the best answer for each of the following:

Q1: Animations are built by connecting a series of:
- a. Tags
- b. Items
- c. Frames

Q2: Disaster recovery includes methods to help systems to recover from:
- a. Outages
- b. Physical damage
- c. Both of these

Q3: Which of the following are features of secure systems?
- a. Firewalls
- b. Clear text passwords
- c. Hard-coded passwords

Assignment: Research a Secure Site

In the real world, securing a site that is high-value, like a bank or wallet, is a race between the professionals who keep the site secure and the hackers who are trying to break into the bank. Choose a website that has the ability to request user credentials such as a login form, sign-in form, and password reset form.

Explore its security mechanisms, including the way the site is protected against hackers on the frontend, according to what you can see from looking at the construction of the forms and using browser developer tools. Then, make some guesses about how the site is protected on the backend, using such things as firewalls, secure handling of sensitive user data, and physical backups. Research if (and how!) this site has ever been hacked (an Internet search can often turn up interesting information).

7. The Whisper Network

Standard: 2-NI-06: Use encryption to secure data for transmission

You settle down to watch the newly gated moss device that you created in Chapter 6, "Securing the Moss," to see if any visitors are able to enter the correct password to gain entrance. You're happy to notice that a line has formed, made up of small black ants, who seem to need to get to the moss. They seem to know the password and gain entrance quickly. What are they up to? And how did they manage to get the password so quickly, given that you just implemented the system?

Being aware of security, break-ins, and hacks, you comment to the Guide, "These ants are up to something suspicious!" "I don't think so," the Guide says with a smile. "Listen!"

You listen attentively and notice a low undercurrent of what can only be described as whispered words and numbers. What on Earth could that be? Bending down, you observe two ants chatting to each other in tiny voices. "What are they saying?" you ask, puzzled. "It's not a language I've ever heard!"

"It's encrypted," replies the Guide. "These ants have developed a sophisticated way to transmit information among the members of their community. No other creature understands what they say, but they seem to be able to tell each other important things such as the gate's password and, most important, the locations of the different patches of this type of moss throughout the forest. They may be an ancient race of creatures, but they use modern encryption to communicate secrets that only they must know. They are the keepers of the moss, you know." You didn't know, actually.

It appears that the moss depends on these ants. The ants help the moss propagate by carrying its spores to new areas of the forest. They are all part of the ecosystem that ensures the moss's survival. "If you could discover what they use to encrypt their messages, you'd be doing me a service," states the Guide. She lifts an ant into her hand and asks it, "Friend, where can we find another patch of moss?" The ant readily tells her, "Xli qsww mw mr xli gezi ex 86.705589 pexmxyhi erh –a5.d9adb7 psrkmxyhi."

Can you crack the ant's code?

Definition

Encryption is the process of converting data into a form that is unreadable by people who do not possess a key to decipher it.

Do Some Research

Since you're learning about encryption, this is a golden opportunity to dive into this rich field of inquiry. People have been trying to keep their messages to each other safe from prying eyes since the dawn of history. One very early example of encrypted communication is the smoke signal, which was used millennia ago, on the Great Wall of China, to send alerts from one turret to another, often using colored smoke.

Ancient Greeks used a method of arranging torches in patterns to signal messages alphabetically. The arrangement of torches represented a number that was converted to a part of the Greek alphabet.

Definition

Cryptography is the study of all the various techniques used to protect messages.

More and more sophisticated ways of encrypting messages have evolved over time. In the information age, powerful computers are available to decrypt and read these encrypted messages. There is always a balance between how sophisticated the encryption is and how quickly the intended user can decrypt and use the message. There is a need to ensure that the messages cannot be decrypted easily by unintended interceptors.

In this chapter, you'll work with an early encryption strategy, the Caesar cipher. There are many more strategies, including the following, which are presented in chronological order, starting with the oldest:

The Caesar Cipher   A cipher that involves shifting letters along a given number of spaces in the alphabet, such that in a Caesar cipher of "shift 2," the letter *a* becomes *c*, and *c* becomes *e*.

The Vigenère Cipher   While a Caesar cipher involves shifting letters along a given number of spaces in the alphabet, a Vigenère cipher is more complex, including several Caesar ciphers with different shift values in a sequence. Rather than a one-line shift along the alphabet, this cipher is represented as a table.

Affine Cipher   This type of cipher is a substitution cipher like the Caesar cipher, except that letters are mapped to corresponding numbers and encrypted with a mathematical function.

M-94 and the Enigma Machine   These were machines used in World Wars I and II to encrypt messages. The M-94 was a cylinder that could be manipulated to create secret messages that were formed and encrypted by aligning letters horizontally. The Enigma machine was used in World War II by the Axis powers. In a more sophisticated version of the M-94, its scrambled letters changed each day, with the order only known to the senders. This made the window for decryption short.

RSA   Named for its inventors, Rivest, Shami, and Adleman, RSA is a modern public-key system in which a public key, used for encryption, is different from a private key, used for decryption. The public key is created by using two large numbers, which are kept secret. Messages can be decoded only by someone with access to both of those numbers. The larger the key, the harder it is to crack the system.

Steganography This is a completely different way of encoding messages. Steganography refers to hiding messages in common formats such as audio, images, or video. Messages can be found when playing audio at a certain volume or video at a certain speed, or by looking at only certain pixels of images. Try an online steganography tool to hide messages in images. These tools allow you to hide a message in an image, save it, and decode it. They do so by subtly attaching extra data to the image's pixels.

Definition

While text can be encrypted using either the *public* or the *private* key, the other key must be used to decrypt the message. Public keys are made available to the public, but only a recipient of a message should have access to and use a private key to decrypt. Learn more about keys at `www.cloudflare.com/learning/ssl/what-is-a-cryptographic-key`.

Do some research on other ways that messages can be encoded and decoded.

Think Like a Computer Scientist: Encryption and Keys

You might wonder how you can put into use a basic cipher such as the one used by Julius Caesar over 2,000 years ago. This cipher is a simple method of encrypting text by shifting each letter by a certain number of places, as shown in Figure 7.1. To decode a message, the reader needs to know that the alphabet order is shifted a given number of places—that's the "key" to decode the message.

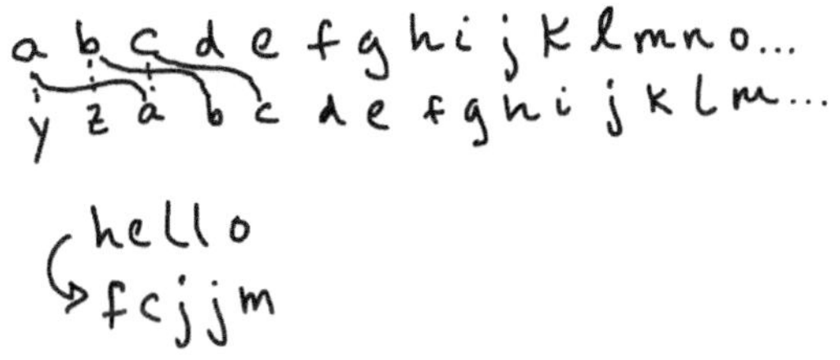

a b c d e f g h i j k l m n o...
y z a b c d e f g h i j k l m...

hello
fcjjm

FIGURE 7.1: A letter-shifted cipher

> **Note**
>
> You'll be able to create a Caesar cipher of your own later in this chapter. Even if it's a simple cipher, it's not so simple to decode it if you don't have a key!

> **Definition**
>
> A *key*, as used for encryption, is a series of numbers used to encrypt or decrypt data. If a key is long and complex, it is more difficult to guess it and thus break an encrypted code. Without a key, it becomes necessary to use various techniques, from "brute-force" guessing to more complex methods, to decrypt a message. Learn more about keys here: `https://phemex.com/academy/what-is-symmetric-key-encryption`.

There are two types of encryption: symmetric encryption and asymmetric encryption. The difference is in their use of keys.

Symmetric encryption relies on a shared secret key to both encrypt and decrypt data. Say, for example, that the key to decrypting a given word is the fact that it is spelled backward. If you know this fact, and the person receiving the encrypted word knows this fact, then the recipient of the word can decode it much faster. There are several different algorithms, some more secure than others and some faster than others, to encrypt data so that a key can help decrypt it efficiently.

Definition

In this context, an *algorithm* is a mathematical formula that converts plain-text messages to encrypted text, also called cyphertext. Learn more about algorithms in cryptography at `https://docs.aws.amazon.com/crypto/latest/userguide/concepts-algorithms.html`.

Asymmetric encryption is the process of encrypting data with a public key and decrypting it with a private key. The public key is shared with the recipient of the data, and the private key is kept secret. The recipient of the data can decrypt the data with the private key but cannot decrypt the data with the public key.

An example of a key would be the Letter + 2 key in the Caesar cipher depicted in Figure 7.1. A more complicated key is depicted in Figure 7.2, where text is encrypted using a Letter + 7 key, such that letters are shifted forward by 7.

While encryption is a useful way to encode messages to protect them, these techniques are not enough to ensure a message's security. There are several elements that need to be considered to enhance security:

- The path from user to server needs to be protected to prevent interception.
- Once data is decrypted, or deciphered for use on a server, other processes need to come into play to continue to protect its integrity.
- The storage of the message on a server needs to also be protected to prevent tampering.

FIGURE 7.2: A Caesar cipher as depicted on criptii.com

Your Challenge

What are the ants telling each other? It's some sort of code, but you don't understand any of it, and neither does your Guide. Your job: determine what kind of encryption they are using and decrypt their message by using a key.

Sketch It Out

Practice both decoding a sample message and then encoding one of your own. Start with the first task. You have a message that you need to decode for the Guide so that she can continue in her role as caretaker of the entire forest. Here is the ant's message again: "Xli qsww mw mr xli gezi ex 86.705589 pexmxyhi erh -a5.d9adb7 psrkmxyhi."

Assume that this is a Caesar cipher, which is characterized by a letter shift. This letter shift value is the key, and your job is to determine the key's value and decode the message. Sketch out the message, the alphabet and numbers you think are included in the code, and a possible letter shift, as can be seen in Figure 7.3. If it's helpful, create two strips of paper and copy the alphabet sequence onto each. You can keep one strip stable and move the other strip to try different letter shifts to determine the key that was used to encrypt the message.

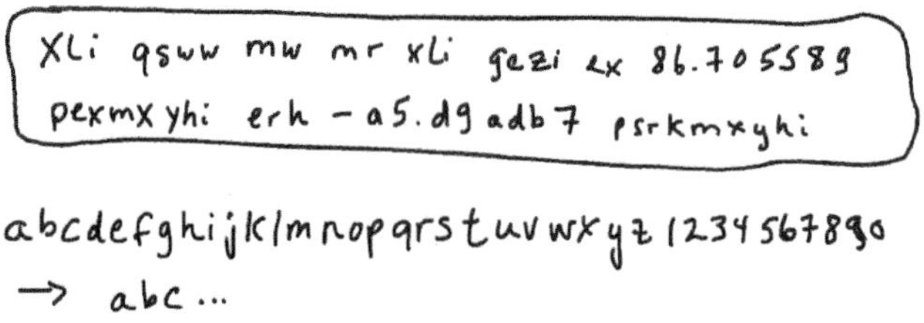

XLi qsww mw mr xLi gezi ex 86.705589
pexmx yhi erh -a5.dg adb7 psrkmxyhi

abcdefghijklmnopqrstuvwxyz 1234567890
→ abc...

FIGURE 7.3: A cipher to decrypt

Project Recipe

You have two tasks before you. First is to decrypt a message for which you have no key, and second, for practice, to encrypt a message with a key and challenge someone to decrypt it. Start by tackling the first, because there are a few ways to approach the problem.

Step 1: Brute Force

Since there are only 26 letters to try, plus the numbers 1,2,3,4,5,6,7,8,9 and 0, and the letters are in the right order, this encrypted message is susceptible to being decoded by what is called brute force. Brute force decryption involves trying one method after another to try to guess an encrypted code's key. In this case, make guesses that start with a presumed key of 1, meaning that A has been shifted to B.

Your first guess might be that the key is 1+. So, A is shifted to B, B to C, and so on. Try the first few letters to see if they make sense. Consider Xli, the first three characters of the code. If the key is 1+, the first letters, decoded, will be wkh. If the key is 2+, it's vjg. If 3+, it's uif. Keep going until the first word makes some sense in English. Does it seem to be using the same shift key if you decode a second word?

104

Step 2: Frequency Analysis

Try a different strategy to crack the code that's slightly better than brute force: frequency analysis. Since this code has breaks between words and the code is presumed to be in English, you can try to see if you can determine patterns based on common words in English that have repeated letters. Think about "is," "the," "an," and "in." Circle repeated letters and try to decipher a pattern as shown in Figure 7.4. Does the word "Xli" correspond in theory to any common three-letter word in English? Is the repeated "i" character a good clue to pursue to figure out other words? Which letters, in English, tend to be repeated often, and which don't? Can that help you rule out some letters, like x and z?

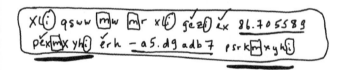

FIGURE 7.4: Attempting to decrypt a cipher

In addition, this code has a peculiarity in that it also includes numbers: 86.705589 and the strange-looking cipher –a5.d9adb7. There is a pattern in these numbers that you might be able to visualize if you break up the words:

```
86.705589 pexmxyhi
erh
-a5.d9adb7 psrkmxyhi
```

Context can help, too! What topic do you think the ants are discussing? Could it have anything to do with moss? Do you see any word in the code that might represent the word "moss"?

Finally, consider how English sentences often begin. What is a common three-letter word that might fit here? The answer to this code is at the end of this chapter, but try to figure it out by yourself!

Step 3: Encrypt a Message

Now it's your turn to encrypt a message. You can continue with a Caesar cipher, or find something more difficult to crack, perhaps a Vigenère or Affine cipher. You can use the tools available for encrypting messages on `https://cryptii.com` or do the encryption by hand.

Try a Vigenère cipher. In this method, the letter shift is done using a key as well as a Vigenère square, or "tabula recta," shown in Figure 7.5.

To do the encryption, imagine you are encrypting the phrase "Preservetheforest." Select a key word such as "guide." Build up the keyword to match the character count of the phrase: "guideguideguidegu."

Use the table to match the phrase horizontally with the first letter of the keyword. So, the first letter, P, matched with G vertically, correlates to V. The next letter, R, matches with U, so the correlation in ciphertext is L. The ciphertext is thus "vlmvixpmwlkzwuiyn." You can see how this cipher is harder to crack, because you now need the table and key to make any sense of it!

Extend Your Knowledge

The history of encryption and cryptography is fascinating and dates back thousands of years. Visit the Bletchley Park website at `https://bletchleypark.org.uk` to learn more about the history of cryptography, in particular during World War II. Bletchley was the location where Alan Turing worked to create machines used to decrypt the German Enigma cipher during World War II. Learn more about Turing and advances in the field of cryptography at the museum website.

```
  a b c d e f g h i j k l m n o p q r s t u v w x y z
a a b c d e f g h i j k l m n o p q r s t u v w x y z
b b c d e f g h i j k l m n o p q r s t u v w x y z a
c c d e f g h i j k l m n o p q r s t u v w x y z a b
d d e f g h i j k l m n o p q r s t u v w x y z a b c
e e f g h i j k l m n o p q r s t u v w x y z a b c d
f f g h i j k l m n o p q r s t u v w x y z a b c d e
g g h i j k l m n o p q r s t u v w x y z a b c d e f
h h i j k l m n o p q r s t u v w x y z a b c d e f g
i i j k l m n o p q r s t u v w x y z a b c d e f g h
j j k l m n o p q r s t u v w x y z a b c d e f g h i
k k l m n o p q r s t u v w x y z a b c d e f g h i j
l l m n o p q r s t u v w x y z a b c d e f g h i j k
m m n o p q r s t u v w x y z a b c d e f g h i j k l
n n o p q r s t u v w x y z a b c d e f g h i j k l m
o o p q r s t u v w x y z a b c d e f g h i j k l m n
p p q r s t u v w x y z a b c d e f g h i j k l m n o
q q r s t u v w x y z a b c d e f g h i j k l m n o p
r r s t u v w x y z a b c d e f g h i j k l m n o p q
s s t u v w x y z a b c d e f g h i j k l m n o p q r
t t u v w x y z a b c d e f g h i j k l m n o p q r s
u u v w x y z a b c d e f g h i j k l m n o p q r s t
v v w x y z a b c d e f g h i j k l m n o p q r s t u
w w x y z a b c d e f g h i j k l m n o p q r s t u v
x x y z a b c d e f g h i j k l m n o p q r s t u v w
y y z a b c d e f g h i j k l m n o p q r s t u v w x
z z a b c d e f g h i j k l m n o p q r s t u v w x y
```

FIGURE 7.5: A Vigenère square

Vocabulary Review

In your own words, describe:

- Cryptography
- Encryption
- Steganography

Quiz

Select the best answer for each of the following:

Q1: Steganography allows you to hide a message in an audio or image file.
   a. True
   b. False

Q2: Symmetric encryption is a method of encrypting data using:
   a. A public key
   b. An NFT
   c. A shared secret key

Q3: Asymmetric encryption is a method of encrypting data using:
   a. Two keys
   b. One private key
   c. One shared key

Assignment: Let's Encrypt

In this chapter, you learned about different methods of encryption used to protect data. Practice your knowledge by converting a message using an encryption technique of your choice and challenging others to decipher it. Research and try:

■ A Caesar cipher
■ A Vigenère cipher
■ Any encryption technique of your choice

The message, encoded, is "The moss is in the cave at 42.361145 latitude and −71.057083 longitude" and the shift is 4+. Did you figure it out?

8. A Well-Tested Solution

Standard: 2-AP-17: Systematically test and refine programs using a range of test cases

Looking back at your work to preserve the moss, you notice how the parts seem to fit together. First, you built a prototype to map out the best route to discover the moss in its hiding place. Then, you built a gate for it and a password strategy so that a user equipped with the proper password would gain access. You also discovered how ants communicate with each other in their own secret code to inform their community about where the patches of moss lie throughout the forest. What if you could bring these parts all together into one larger solution to create a robust strategy to safeguard the rare glowing moss for all future generations?

"It's a lot to think about," admits your Guide when you mention this idea. "What if one part doesn't work well? Will everything else then fail? It seems like you should stop to think about all the things that might fail and build a plan to test them. By having a plan, you make sure that all the parts of the system work together."

"I'll build a testing plan!" you say, agreeing that this is an interesting idea. You start looking at the ways that testing can help you think about your projects as part of a larger system of parts that all need to fit together.

> **Note**
>
> Did you know that problems in software were most famously termed "bugs" by Grace Hopper, a famous computer programmer in the first half of the 20th century who liked to tell the story that a moth caught in a hardware system she was working on caused a software glitch—the world's first computer bug.

Do Some Research

To get into the practice of testing a simple system, do some research on the various ways to test. In general, there are a number of types of tests, including unit tests, regression tests, integration tests, and system tests.

Unit tests are designed to test a single piece (or unit) of an application, like a login form. This type of test is usually automated. If the testing framework finds a bug, the unit fails. If the software is bug-free, it passes the test.

Once tests are passing, they can be saved to perform *regression testing*, which can catch bugs that appear after the software changes at a later date. Since software often evolves a lot over its life span, regression testing is important to make sure that the software remains bug-free even if parts of it change over time. Once individual unit tests pass consistently, you can combine them to perform *integration testing*, which tests a larger group of software parts, like an entire signup, login, and password reset routine.

Once the integration tests pass, an entire *system test* can be run on all the disparate parts of an application.

Research the difference between manual and automated testing. You can watch some examples of how they are accomplished on YouTube.

Think Like a Computer Scientist

From a systems standpoint, software engineers and computer scientists are highly concerned with problems in software. Not all bugs, faults, and failures are mistakes made by programmers; they occur because of a missed requirement, a design flaw, a missed connection between frontend and backend systems, or something else. Take a minute to think about all the ways that mistakes can occur in a software or hardware system and how testing can help uncover potential problems.

Sketch It Out

In Chapters 5, "Goblin's Gold," and 6, "Securing the Moss," you built two prototypes to safeguard and password-protect access to some endangered moss. In Chapter 7, "The Whisper Network," you cracked a decrypted code that gives information about the moss's password to a select community, Now, bring it all together as a system where your maze program leads to a gated area that can only be opened by a password encrypted so that ants can understand it. Since you are building a testing plan, circle and notate the elements that need to be tested as part of this system and consider fallbacks or failovers—points where your users can go if part of a system fails. Your sketch might look like Figure 8.1.

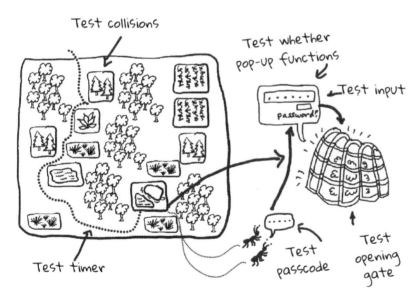

FIGURE 8.1: A sketch of the system with tests

Your Challenge

Now that you've sketched a test suite for your simple Secure Moss system prototype, start thinking about how you would build a test suite to find its weak spots.

One interesting thing about software testing as a discipline is that it helps programmers actually write better-quality code. A programmer can write a test for a piece of code, and then write the code to build the system. First, the test is run on simple code, and as it passes or fails, the code is refactored or rewritten to eventually allow it to meet its use case. So, your job is to write use cases and test scenarios. In the project recipe that follows, you don't have to write the actual tests or code (unless you want to!), but you can create a rubric as if you were a programmer working on building up your complex system that's reinforced by solid testing.

Definition

In software development, a *use case* is a given scenario that is managed by a piece of software. Use cases are used to determine the requirements of a system. A given web page, for example, must not be accessed by the general public, so a use case for a login form with authentication is defined to describe the various elements of this scenario.

Project Recipe

In this project, you'll be building a full test plan to help test the various possible failure points of your gated system.

Step 1: Build a Testing List

Write down a list of the parts of your system that need to be tested. You can divide it into three parts: the maze, the password, and the gate system. A list of what to test in these three sections might look, in part, like this:

a. Maze

- Lives are decremented correctly on each collision.
- Only player lives are decremented if a collision occurs between the player and a deciduous tree
- Ensure that the game ends when the player has no more lives left.
- The timer decrements from 10 seconds to 0 seconds properly.
- The game ends if the timer runs out and a pop-up states "game over."
- The game can be won in the given time frame as long as the player has lives left.

b. Password

- The password request pops up when the player approaches the moss area.
- The password request form only accepts an agreed-upon encoded password.
- The input password is limited in length, and it is not possible to input more characters than the specified maximum length.
- The password is required.
- If the password is input incorrectly, the user is prompted to try again.

c. Gate

- The gate only opens if the password is correct.
- The gate closes again within a few seconds.

Step 2: Build a Test Scenario Table

Now, build a table based on the list you built in Step 1. The table should include a use case and a scenario for how you want to test the use case. Table 2.1 presents a sample of use cases selected from the list in Step 1, focusing specifically on the password input area.

TABLE 2.1: Tests for the system

Use Case	Test scenario
An ant approaches the moss enclosure and attempts to input a password.	Test that the password must be required and of a given length.
The gate's password system displays a window on approach.	Test that the pop-up window is able to pop up to show the password system, handles a password error as an error message, and can be closed and reopened manually.
A password is correctly input.	Test that the gate opens if the password is input correctly.
The password is incorrectly entered.	Test that the error is handled as a visual alert.

Step 3: Get Set Up to Test

Now it's your turn to run an actual test that tests a password system that is built as a sample into this book's website. Visit `https://cs4kids.club/passcode` to see a site that contains a password sample that you'll test. You can imagine this web page is a way to input a password for the gated system you're designing.

To do the testing, you'll be using a testing framework called Playwright (`https://playwright.dev`) that helps set up unit tests to check whether all the elements of your system are working as expected.

To begin, visit `https://github.com/cs4kids/Sample-Test`. If you don't already have a GitHub account, you can create one for free.

> **Note**
>
> If you are under the age of 13, you will need a teacher, parent, or adult mentor to complete this step and the following instructions using Codespaces, as GitHub's terms of service do not apply to users younger than 13.

114

In this folder, you'll find code that has been configured to use Playwright's testing library to test a website. If you navigate to the tests folder in this repository, you'll find a file called `passcode.spec.ts`. This is a file that contains a bit of code that tests for a few things in the password sample on `http://cs4kids.club`. You should be able to run the test in your browser using a tool called Codespaces, which is a way to use GitHub without having to download anything to your computer.

> **Note**
>
> While you can run tests using Codespaces, you can also make a copy of this Sample-Test code and run tests on your own computer. The easiest way is to download a zip file of the code and open it using Visual Studio Code (VS Code), a free code editor that you can download at `https://vscode.dev`. If you install the Playwright VS Code extension found at `https://marketplace.visualstudio.com/items?itemName=ms-playwright.playwright`, running tests can be done from the "beaker" icon in the left navigation. For this chapter, however, you can use Codespaces.

Open a Codespace by clicking the green Code button in GitHub and using the Codespaces tab in the drop-down that appears, as shown in Figure 8.2. Click Create codespace on main to start working in the browser.

Now you are ready to start working in the browser with this code.

Step 4: Install the Playwright Extension

Before getting started with Playwright, you need to install an extension, or an extra library, into Codespace, the online coding environment you just opened. Click the Extensions icon (it looks like boxes) on the left navigation and search for Playwright. The extension will look like Figure 8.3.

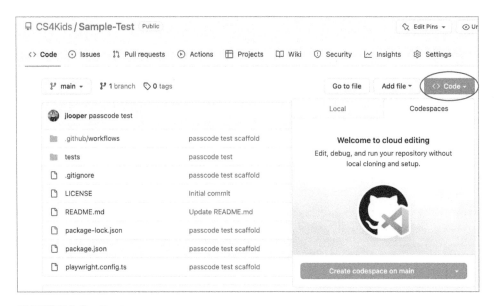

FIGURE 8.2: Codespaces
Source: GitHub, Inc.

FIGURE 8.3: Playwright extension in VS Code
Source: GitHub, Inc.

Install the extension in your Codespace by clicking the green Install in Codespaces extension. A Testing icon appears in the left navigation, and when you click it, the test folder is visible.

Before you can run a test, there's one more thing you need to do. Your browser window should look like Figure 8.4, with a terminal available at the bottom right of the screen.

> **Definition**
>
> A *terminal* is either a window in your code editor or an application on your computer that allows you to run commands. In this case, you'll use it to further set up your workspace for testing.

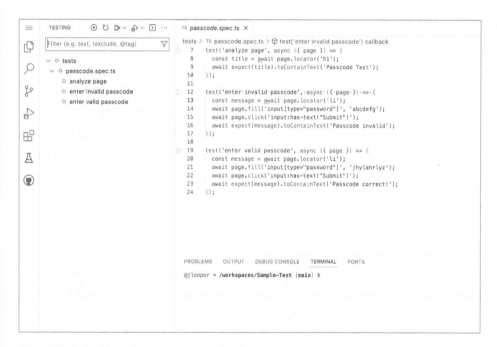

FIGURE 8.4: Your browser as a Codespace

Source: GitHub, Inc.

> **Note**
>
> If a terminal isn't visible, go to the File Explorer by clicking the top file icon in the left navigation. Click the ellipsis (three lines) icon at the top and choose Terminal ➤ New Terminal. At the $ prompt, type `npx playwright install`. This command installs some browser emulators to let you test on several different browsers in the background. Once this installation completes, you are ready to run your tests.

Step 5: Run a Test with Playwright

Open the test folder and expand the `passcode.spec.ts` file, where you'll find several tests. You can see the entire test code by holding your mouse over a test's name and clicking Go To Test.

Hold your mouse over the `passcode.spec.ts` filename and click the arrow to start running tests. Some passing and failing tests look like what is shown in Figure 8.5.

What's going on here? The test software is opening a web page, looking for elements in its code, checking behaviors, and seeing if all is working as expected. You can edit the code in this test in the Codespace and retry any failing test or write a new test. See if you can build a test to check for a different behavior, such as entering too many characters.

Congratulations! You've built a testing plan and run some tests against a portion of a pretty complex system. Well done!

Did you notice that the password is a cipher: jhylahrlyz? Can you decipher the ant's password? As a hint, it's a Caesar cipher with a 7+ key. You can use Cryptii (`https://cryptii.com/pipes/caesar-cipher`) or your paper decoder to determine the plain-text meaning of this cipher.

FIGURE 8.5: Passing and failing tests

Source: GitHub, Inc.

Extend Your Knowledge

There are other types of testing besides test-driven development (TDD). Do some research on the types of software development that are paired with testing, such as behavior-driven development (BDD), feature-driven development (FDD), and acceptance test–driven development (ATDD). Each of these requires different patterns of testing and software development. Which seems most logical to you?

Vocabulary Review

In your own words, describe:

■ Integration test
■ Regression test

- System test
- Unit test

Quiz

Select the best answer for each of the following:

Q1: Which one of these is a testing framework?
- a. Playful
- b. Playpretty
- c. Playwright

Q2: TDD stands for:
- a. Taco-driven development
- b. Test-driven development
- c. Training-driven development

Q3: A test can uncover faults in coding logic.
- a. True
- b. False

Assignment: Time to Test

Now that you have practiced designing a test suite for your Secure Moss prototype, create a five-part test suite outline for a system in real life. Find a website that you can test. Think about the elements on the site that would benefit from having a solid test behind them. An example would be a login form on `Fidelity.com`, which has several fields and a button to log in. Even a simple form could have many tests to check for the integrity of the form. Use the worksheet on our website to build a suite for one element of a public-facing website.

III
Geode Quest

9. Searching for Geodes

Standard: 2-DA-07: Represent data using multiple encoding schemes

"Now that you're well on your way to becoming our newest Forest Defender," says the Guide, "you're ready to start working with endangered species and the data that they generate and consume." She starts walking along the stream where the moss grows thickly. You follow her lead, noticing in passing that the stream trickles merrily over many round-shaped stones. Some stones are worn and smooth, others have sharp edges, while still others have curious bumps and knobs. A particularly knobby stone with a chalky exterior catches your eye, and you pick it up. "What kind of stones are these?" you ask your Guide.

"There are many types, and it is our job as Forest Defenders to make sure they are not misplaced or stolen," notes the Guide. You come to a bend in the creek and stop. "Each year we take inventory of the stones that gather in this bend. Most valuable are the geodes, and we guard them carefully."

As you watch, the Guide takes the stone that you picked up, places it on a flat boulder, and taps it sharply several times with another stone. It breaks in half, revealing a stunning array of purple crystals inside. The colors shimmer and glint in the sunshine. "You see? Collectors love to come and take these beautiful geodes. They tramp through our forest and take all they can find. I suppose they crack them open and sell them. Because the stream moves the stones around, it's hard to tell how many they take and how many remain. Can you help us determine how many geodes there are among all these various stones, and perhaps categorize the other types of stones that remain? In this way, our yearly inventory task will be so much easier and faster to accomplish!"

You readily agree to take on the job of differentiating the geodes in this riverbed from the plain stones and sorting them into some type of logical structure. Maybe, if the Guide is pleased, she will give you a geode of your own.

Do Some Research

Accomplishing the job will involve two steps. First, you will need to research how you can tell the difference between geodes and other types of stones. Second, you need to think about the ways stones can be sorted.

Questions to think about include:

- What do geodes look like?
- What is a geode's chemical composition?
- In what types of geologic deposits are geodes typically found?
- How can they be differentiated from other types of stones without cracking them open?
- What types of stones are often found around geode deposits?

Once you have an understanding of geodes and their surrounding stones, your next task is to think of all the ways you could sort the stones into a logical structure to build an inventory.

Brainstorm the ways that you could organize all these stones. You can never be quite sure that a stone is a geode without opening it, so you need to determine which aspects of a stone make it most likely to be a geode and then sort the group accordingly.

Think Like a Computer Scientist

Computer scientists who work with the web or with data science spend a lot of time thinking about how to best sort and organize data.

What is *data*, exactly? It depends on the context. In computer science, data is information that you can use to make predictions or decisions. It can come in all shapes, sizes, and formats, and it's up to a computer scientist specializing in data—a data scientist—to figure out how to best analyze it, shape it, and use it to answer pressing questions. You'll explore the craft of a data scientist in the next chapter.

An engineer building a search utility, for example, needs to sort through a huge set of potential search results to determine the best match. Consider what decisions both frontend and backend engineers need to make to determine the sort order.

The *frontend* of a website is the user interface, where people can interact with the site's graphic elements such as drop-downs, buttons, and checkboxes. The *backend* is where a website's data is stored.

A developer working on the frontend of a website needs to think about how to organize and present data in the most user-friendly way. Think about a travel website. How do you think the designers and developers organized the way information is presented on a screen? How about when they had to build a checkout form for buying a plane ticket?

Now, consider the backend of this travel website. Developers who work with databases work closely with designers to develop the database, a place where data needs to be stored to support this website. In the case of a travel site, a database would need to store information about available tickets, the people who buy them, and much more. To do this, a database developer must carefully design the various areas where data is stored.

Often, data is stored in *tables* made up of rows of information that categorize elements that are set in the table's column heading. For example, a table containing plane ticket information might include rows of information including a ticket's ID, the flight number, the air carrier, the time of departure, the time of landing, and the ticket price. It's often important to include a unique ID in a table with each row of information (or row of ticket information in this case) so that other tables can connect (or be *joined*) to it. For example, a plane ticket table might join the ticket ID to a separate table containing the purchaser's information. Designing a good database structure that can work well as more data is added to its tables is the job of a database developer, sometimes also called a database administrator, or DBA.

> Note
>
> In software development, you'll often find tabular data stored in an array, a data structure that can store data as rows and, sometimes, columns.

Sketch It Out

Before working with data, it's useful to draw a picture of the data you're working with and envision how you'd lay it out in a table. Create a table using pencil and paper, showing the various columns of your inventory of geodes and stones. What features do you want to list to represent this inventory? Your sketch might look like Figure 9.1.

Your Challenge

In this challenge, you will investigate different ways to organize your geologic inventory by using different tools to perform the task. This task is best accomplished by using tools such as Microsoft Excel, Google Sheets, and text editors. Finally, you will dive deeper into the many ways that you can "express your data" using different kinds of encoding.

Id	Name	Desc	Weight	Size	Color	Lat	Long	Image
1		...	2	2	Gray	49	-29	
2	...	...	1.2	14	Red	46	-25	
3	...	...	3.4	2.4	Blk	44	-22	
4	...	...	5	6	Gray	41	-23	
5	...	...	6.2	1.4	Red	42	-20	
6	...	...	2.2	5	Brn	40	-21	
7	...	...	2	5.1	Red	41	-20	

FIGURE 9.1: Your sketch of the inventory

Definition

Encoding is the process of converting data into a standard format for storage and transmission.

Project Recipe

For this project, you're going to practice using the tools of a software engineer or data scientist to organize data. Imagine that you are looking at a pile of stones and you hope to be able to determine how many of them might be geodes. How would you go about doing it? You could create an inventory of all the stones by size, shape, and color. Then, you could find a way to determine which stones in the pile have the traits of a geode.

Consider that geodes usually have the following traits:

- Have a lower mass than their size would suggest, because they are hollow
- Are usually spherical
- Are usually bumpy in texture
- Are often gray in color with a white, chalky outer coating

Step 1: Build an Inventory Using a Spreadsheet

Pick a spreadsheet software program and start building a sample inventory of the stones you might see in a creek bed.

Definition

A *spreadsheet* is a file format that allows you to organize data in tables, usually in rows and columns. Examples include Microsoft Excel and Google Sheets, both of which can be used online.

Start by considering the column headings that you might use. These could be Size, Shape, Color, Weight, Hardness, Crust, Texture, and so on. Give each stone a unique identifier in a column labeled something like **Stone_Id**. This gives each stone a unique ID so it can be more easily identified. Add some sample data for each of the columns.

Definition

You might come across the terms *data* and *dataset* as you start to work with spreadsheets and tables. While data refers to all types of information, when data is collected and organized into a usable format, a dataset is created. While you're building your spreadsheet, you're gathering data to form a dataset.

128

Think about how you want to describe your data. For size, you want to deter-mine a standard way to measure the stones, for example the diameter (the length of the stone, measured straight across) or the circumference (the meas-urement around the stone) in centimeters (cm). Think carefully about your column-naming strategy. For example, if you are referring to your items by their diameter, maybe you should rename the Size column to Diameter to avoid confusion.

> **Note**
>
> Naming things effectively can be really hard in software development. Some engineers say it's the hardest thing of all to do!

Engineers use standard naming conventions when working with data so that their code is self-explanatory. For example, naming a column representing the diameter of a stone in centimeters **Column 1** is not a good idea because another person will have a difficult time understanding the meaning of the data. Instead, choose a convention such as using underscores to separate words in column names, using something like **Diameter_cm** consistently. That way, your columns will follow a naming pattern such as "Description + underscore + unit of measure" and your code will be easier to read and understand. Don't for-get to make your capitalization consistent, too! With this idea in mind, edit your spreadsheet to use the convention you've chosen. It might resemble Figure 9.2.

> **Definition**
>
> *Refactoring* is the process of revising your code to make it more efficient and easier to read.

	A	B	C	D	E
1	Rock_id	Diameter_cm	Shape_desc	Color_desc	Weight_pounds
2	1	20	spherical	black	10
3	2	12	square	red	13
4	3	47	triangle	black	4.4
5	4	66	spherical	red	10
6	5	56	square	black	5
7	6	45	triangle	red	3.5
8	7	55	spherical	black	6.7
9	8	20	square	red	5.9
10	9	90	triangle	black	3
11	10	10	spherical	red	6
12					

FIGURE 9.2: A spreadsheet with sample data about a stone inventory

Step 2: Use Your Spreadsheet to Build a Graph

Most spreadsheet programs offer tools to help you build graphs so that you can visualize your data. A picture is worth a thousand words, and graphs allow you to see patterns that otherwise would be hard to see. If you're working in Google sheets, select **create** ➤ **chart** in the menu bar, and use the Chart editor to choose the columns you want to visualize. In Excel, choose **Insert (Recommended)** ➤ **Chart**. In this example, we selected the data range **B1:E11**.

In the editor, we chose to compare the size and weight of the stones, removing the `Stone_Id` column as it is not needed for this graph. The result is a graph that shows the relationship between the size and weight of the stones, as shown in Figure 9.3. Most of the stones are quite heavy, given their diameter. Since geodes are usually light for their size because they are hollow, it is unlikely that those particular stones are geodes. Conversely, particularly light stones, given their diameter, might be worth focusing on as potential geodes. Three stones are lighter, given their circumference. These three might warrant further investigation. By adding labels to the columns, you can discover that two of the three geode candidates are spherical, so they very well might be geodes!

130

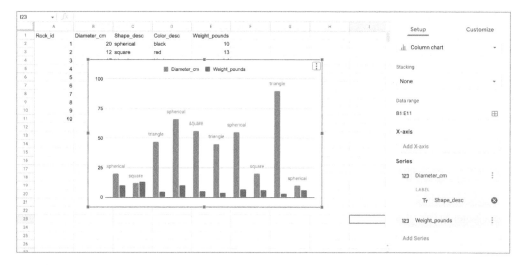

FIGURE 9.3: A sample chart from a spreadsheet
Source: Microsoft Corporation.

Step 3: Try Different Encoding Techniques on Your Data

If you look at your color column, you note that you are only listing a one-word description of a stone color: red or black, for example. These words are what could be termed "high-level abstraction"—a term that can be applied to many contexts. What if you know that geodes have a particular external color, and you want to provide a more precise representation of the actual color without adding a lot of descriptive text to your data?

You might turn to a "low-level" abstraction that can give more specific details by its format about a given color. Fortunately, there are good ways to encode colors into a low-level system of numbers or letters plus numbers. In these systems, the color "light cornflower blue" can be translated to 153,204,234 or #93CCEA. This is done by using encoding schemes used by programmers to represent color.

Visit the site `https://color-hex.com` or `https://colorhexa.com`. On these sites you can search for the color red and discover several encoding schemes that programmers can use to represent the various saturations of the color. While you can use colors by their official names (such as red, glacial blue ice, or slate gray) in your web projects, there are two particularly common ways to express color as numbers via encoding: RGB and hex.

In styling a website, you might come across an RGB value for a color. RGB refers to red, green, and blue and uses a scale of values from 0 to 255 to specify how much red, green, or blue a given color includes. Pure red is represented as 255,0,0 in the RGB system, as it has only red and no other colors mixed in.

Hexadecimal, or hex, is an encoding that uses a base 16 number system. While it is used for various purposes in programming, in this context it is used by websites to determine colors.

Computers tend to rely on decimals, or base 10, to represent bytes of data—the numbers 0 to 9. The hexadecimal system builds on this by using 16 values: the numbers 0 to 9 plus six more values. The numbers 10 to 15 are represented with the letters A through F. This system converts the 0–255 values to correspond to a combination of numbers and letters by dividing a base 10 number by 16 until there is no remainder. For example, converting light cornflower blue from its RGB value of 147,204,234 to hex involves the following steps:

- Convert 147 to its hexadecimal equivalent value: 93
- Convert 204 to its hexadecimal equivalent value: CC
- Convert 243 to its hexadecimal equivalent value: F0

Combining these three individual color pieces results in the hex number of 93CCF0, which can be represented with a hash sign to signal it is a hex code: #93CCF0.

> **Note**
>
> You can try this conversion method using online converters at websites such as `www.rapidtables.com/convert/number/base-converter.html`.

Step 4: Refactoring for Precision

Edit your spreadsheet to reflect the actual color of your stones. Look at real stones in your area to figure out their various shades of brown, black, and gray and translate those colors into either the RGB system or the hex system and add those values to your spreadsheet. By looking for a particular shade, could you guess whether or not a stone is a geode? Your spreadsheet will now look like Figure 9.4.

	A	B	C	D	E	F
1	Rock_id	Diameter_cm	Shape_desc	Color_hex	Color_desc	Weight_pounds
2	1	20	spherical	#000000	black	10
3	2	12	square	#FF0000	red	13
4	3	47	triangle	#000000	black	4.4
5	4	66	spherical	#FF0000	red	10
6	5	56	square	#000000	black	5
7	6	45	triangle	#FF0000	red	3.5
8	7	55	spherical	#000000	black	6.7
9	8	20	square	#FF0000	red	5.9
10	9	90	triangle	#000000	black	3
11	10	10	spherical	#FF0000	red	6
12						

FIGURE 9.4: Your final spreadsheet

Extend Your Knowledge

Quantifying data around real-life objects is a struggle for many different types of professionals. Museum curators, for example, have to think about how to describe the many aspects of their collections as elaborate datasets. Explore some interesting real-world datasets on sites like `Kaggle.com` to see how people handle "data wrangling" in the real world. In the next lesson, we'll turn to some manipulation of actual geological data to see how we can clean it for use.

Vocabulary Review

In your own words, describe:

- Data
- Dataset
- Hexadecimal
- High-level vs. low-level abstraction
- RGB
- Spreadsheet
- Table

Quiz

Select the best answer for each of the following:

Q1: The hexadecimal color #FFFFFF represents:
   a. Black
   b. White
   c. Red

Q2: A database often includes tabular data.
   a. True
   b. False

Q3: Spreadsheets are most useful for:
   a. Visualizing data
   b. Querying data
   c. Organizing data in a table format

Assignment: Representing Data

Data can be represented in many different ways. Geodes, for example, come in many shapes and forms, with different types of crystals inside. Colors can be represented by RGB or hex, and sizes can be represented by millimeters or centimeters. Give five examples of a thing that can be represented in different ways. Use the downloadable worksheet to organize your work. Be sure to include both a low-level and a high-level representation of a given value, such as colors.

10. Cleaning and Categorizing the Collection

Standard: 2-DA-08: Collect data using computational tools and transform the data to make it more useful and reliable

Down on your hands and knees in the dirt next to the stream, you spend several hours sifting through the pile of rocks, noting their color, weighing them, and trying not to disturb their placement so that you can accurately note their position in the stream. With the help of some obliging frogs who live in the stream, you start building a catalog of the stones as a table, with each stone listed by weight, size, placement, color, and other attributes. Rapidly inputting data, you discover that you have amassed a sizable amount of information. Pausing for breath, you look at your work.

Dismayed, you notice that your table of data has grown large but has gaps, inconsistencies, missing values, and other errors. Maybe you shouldn't have worked so quickly, or maybe you were tired and made mistakes. Maybe the rocks you categorized as brown are only brown when wet but turn a chalky gray when dry.

"Don't worry," says your Guide, noticing your expression. "There are good ways to clean up your data, and we can help you do it. In the process, you'll also be able to discover some interesting facts about our rock collection and how the stones relate to each other." The helpful frogs nod wisely, croaking "Rub it, rub it" as an encouragement to you to clean up the data.

Do Some Research

In this chapter, you'll continue to work directly with data, which are best handled in spreadsheets, databases, and other similar tools. While the results might be less exciting visually, they are nonetheless satisfying as your data collection grows, evolves, and reveals its secrets. In this chapter you'll put on the hat of a data scientist and explore some of the tools that you'll need to work with your data.

Do some research on the common tools and processes of a data scientist. For example, where do they get their data in the real world? How do they clean it up? How do they analyze it? How do they visualize it? What software do they use most often to work with their data?

Think Like a Computer Scientist

Data scientists are "data wranglers," computer scientists who specialize in working with data. Their primary goal is to gather datasets—large collections of data—and analyze them to find insights and patterns that they can use to make decisions. Think about the kinds of decisions that can be made by a data scientist observing patterns in data:

- When to restock shelves in a grocery store based on the availability of certain items
- When to buy a new car based on the way that cars of its type tend to age
- How much to expect to pay for a house based on its location
- How a costume museum's collection evolved based on fashions over the years
- The type of emergency assistance calls people make based on their location

What other questions can be answered by a careful data analysis?

Your Challenge

The first task of a data scientist is to clean and then visualize data. You can do this right in a browser environment or on your local computer, using Jupyter notebooks.

> **Note**
>
> *Jupyter notebooks* are interactive files that you can open in a code editor such as Visual Studio Code, edit, and then run, code cell by code cell. They also contain a space where you can add text to explain the various sections of code.

Since data science tends to require a reasonable amount of data (more than you probably included in your sample spreadsheet from the previous chapter), you can use a dataset that is available online that includes about 500 rock samples taken by scientists from Antarctica.

Your job will be to clean this data and then create a chart to visualize it. Similar to the rock collection in the creek that you catalogued, this dataset includes information about the types of rock that are found in this location, their description, location, and weight.

> **Note**
>
> Jupyter notebook files have the file extension `.ipynb`. They are a great way to organize your data science work into a self-documented file that can organize your analyses into a readable format.

Project Recipe

In this project, you will use Kaggle (`https://kaggle.com`) from a web browser. Kaggle is a free data science platform that lets you upload and analyze data. Kaggle is also where you will find the data for the rock samples. You'll be working with some data about polar rocks that's already on Kaggle to experiment with completing some data science tasks.

> **Note**
>
> To save your work on Kaggle, you will need to create an account and log in. Students under the age of 13 are not allowed to use Kaggle, so this chapter should be done with the help of a parent or guardian if you are younger than 13. In general, for younger students, it's best to use Kaggle under the supervision of a parent, guardian, or teacher.

Step 1: Create a New Notebook

Go to `https://kaggle.com`. Once on the Kaggle site, you will need to register to create an account if you don't already have one. Once your account has been created, log in to get to the Kaggle work area. To create a notebook to use for this project, click **Create** ➤ **New Notebook**. Your new notebook will resemble Figure 10.1.

FIGURE 10.1: A Kaggle notebook

Source: Kaggle, Inc.

140

Step 2: Import Data

On the upper right side of the screen, click **Add data** and search for **500 Polar Rocks**. When the dataset is found, click **Add** to add the data into your notebook's environment, as in Figure 10.2.

FIGURE 10.2: Importing the rock dataset

Source: Kaggle, Inc.

Click the small **Run** button (▷) to the left of the code cell that is included in the notebook. After a short wait, your data is added to your notebook, and you can start working with it. You can see that the notebook session has been started and the data has been added and is ready to be used in the notebook because the name of the data file now shows under the code cell, as shown in Figure 10.3.

FIGURE 10.3: Adding the polar rock data

Source: Kaggle, Inc.

Step 3. Display Your Data

Now that you have imported your data, it's time to work with it. What does it look like? To analyze your data, you can use a handy library called pandas. Create a new code cell in your notebook by clicking the **+ Code** button at the bottom of your screen and then import the pandas library to display your data by typing this code into the new cell:

```
import pandas as pd
data = pd.read_csv("../input/polar-rocks/prr_search_results
.csv")
data.head()
```

142

By using the pandas `head()` function, you display the first five rows of the data. As Figure 10.4 shows, the data is in a tabular format with 24 columns.

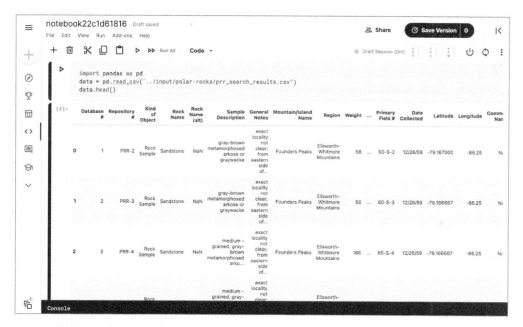

FIGURE 10.4: The displayed rock data

Source: Kaggle, Inc.

What do you observe about this data? Are there columns that are not useful? You only want a basic set of columns for your inventory. It is likely not useful for your inventory to include the Kind of Object, Rock Name (alt), General Notes, Mountain/Island Name, and other extra columns.

Step 4: Drop Unneeded Data

You can drop the columns you don't need, such as the columns mentioned in the previous section. You can always add them back later by editing the drop column code and rerunning the notebook. Add a code cell to your notebooks by clicking the **+ Code** button. You can drop columns from your pandas data frame by entering one line of code in your new cell:

```
data.drop(data.columns[[1,2,4,6,7,8]], axis=1,
inplace=True)
```

Once you click the **Run** button to the left of the cell, you will see that several columns get dropped. If you want to drop more columns, add their indexes between the brackets in the code, or the numbers of their columns, noting that the column index count begins at 0.

Definition

In this context, the *index* refers to a given place in an array of numbers. In an array of numbers like [1,2,3,4,5], the array's index at 0 is the number 1. In the case of the data in Figure 10.4, if Database # is at index 0 and Repository # is at 1, what is the index of Region?

View your edited data frame by adding another line to your current code cell to see its first five rows. Type **data.head()** on this line, and then rerun the whole notebook by selecting the Run All button at the top. In this way, you can refresh the notebook and see your data frame in its new form as shown in Figure 10.5.

144

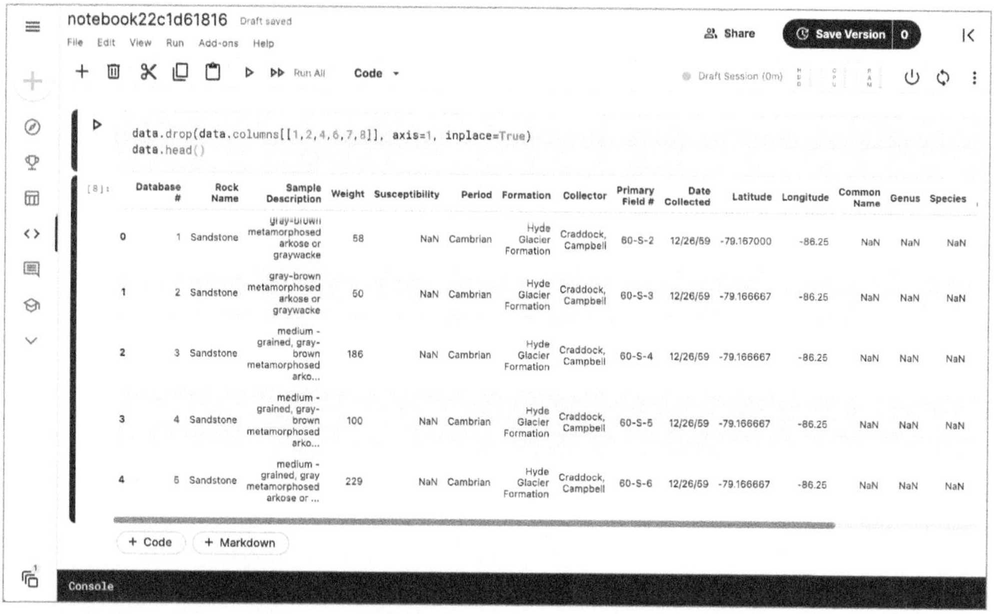

FIGURE 10.5: The refined rock data

Source: Kaggle, Inc.

Step 5: Handle Missing Values

Looking at your data, you can see that there are problematic values, listed as NaN (Not a Number). This indicates that you're missing data, and that's not helpful for your task of evaluating your rock collection. Instead of dropping columns, try dropping rows where any data is missing by creating a new code cell as you did before and adding the following code that drops any row that has missing data:

```
data = data.dropna()
data
```

Notice that your data frame is now empty! This dataset contains no rows that are fully populated. Roll back that change by deleting the previous code from its cell and rerunning the entire notebook by selecting the **Run All** button at the top.

Since this dataset has a lot of missing data, you need to make a decision on whether to drop columns where there is *any* missing data or only drop columns that have *mostly* missing data.

Try dropping all columns where there is *any* missing data. Do this by specifying that you are dropping columns using the parameter `axis='columns'`. Add the following code to a new cell and run it:

```
data = data.dropna(axis='columns')
data
```

This result probably reduces your data frame too much, as now you have lost the interesting Sample Description and Formation columns. Your data frame now looks like Figure 10.6.

```
data = data.dropna(axis='columns')
data
```

[9]:		Database #	Rock Name	Weight	Collector	Primary Field #	Date Collected	Latitude	Longitude
	0	1	Sandstone	58	Craddock, Campbell	60-S-2	12/26/59	-79.167000	-86.250
	1	2	Sandstone	50	Craddock, Campbell	60-S-3	12/26/59	-79.166667	-86.250
	2	3	Sandstone	186	Craddock, Campbell	60-S-4	12/26/59	-79.166667	-86.250
	3	4	Sandstone	100	Craddock, Campbell	60-S-5	12/26/59	-79.166667	-86.250
	4	5	Sandstone	229	Craddock, Campbell	60-S-6	12/26/59	-79.166667	-86.250
	...	...	...	...	...	...	...	...	...
	494	497	Limestone	62	Webers, Gerald	63-W-207D	12/9/62	-79.735000	-83.943
	495	498	Marble	774	Webers, Gerald	63-W-207E	12/9/62	-79.735000	-83.943
	496	499	Quartzite	340	Webers, Gerald	63-W-207J	12/9/62	-79.735000	-83.943
	497	500	Quartzite	177	Webers, Gerald	63-W-207K	12/9/62	-79.735000	-83.943
	498	501	Quartzite	163	Webers, Gerald	63-W-207L	12/9/62	-79.735000	-83.943

499 rows × 8 columns

FIGURE 10.6: A reduced data frame
Source: Kaggle, Inc.

Try fine-tuning your data frame by dropping columns where there is *mostly* missing data. Edit your previous column to include a threshold of 200, which

146

allows some blank data to exist in the column. Rerun the entire notebook one more time using the **Run All** button at the top after entering the following:

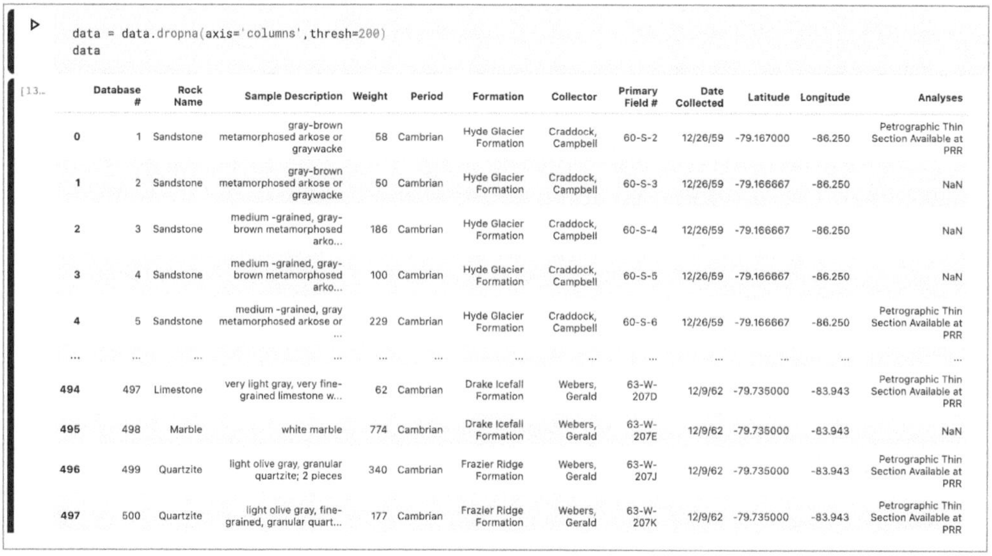

```
data = data.dropna(axis='columns', thresh=200)
data
```

By setting the threshold of a minimum amount of data that a column needs to have (in the previous code, you need to have a minimum of 200 rows available), you have kept some more data with which to work. Your data frame now looks like Figure 10.7.

FIGURE 10.7: A workable data frame

Source: Kaggle, Inc.

Step 6: Tidy Up the Decimals

One more thing you might do is to change the decimals of the data so that the values can be more easily compared. Notice that in the Latitude and Longitude columns, decimals are of different lengths. Add a new cell to your notebook with the following code:

```
data = data.round(2)
data
```

> **Note**
>
> Be careful when rounding numbers in data. While your data will be neater, you just changed the true Latitude and Longitude of your rocks, which might be a problem later on.

This code searches the data frame for decimals to round to two spaces, so that, for example, 7.678 is converted to 7.68. Feel free to try other rounding values. When you run the cell, you'll find that the Latitude and Longitude columns are neater now.

> **Tip**
>
> A good way to remember how rounding works is the phrase "five and above, give it a shove, four and below, let it go."

> **Note**
>
> What other columns would you change? What if you wanted to change the way a sample's weight is measured, or change the way dates are formatted? You can find out how to do this by reading through the pandas documentation at `https://pandas.pydata.org`.

Step 7: Visualize the Data

When you're satisfied with its format you can start to visualize your data, or represent it in charts or graphs to more easily understand it. This is a very fun and interesting aspect of data science, and it's helpful to be able to do it using various libraries that you can import into your notebook.

> **Note**
>
> In Chapter 9, "Searching for Geodes," you visualized data in a spreadsheet that allows the creation of graphs and charts. Now you can use Python to build some interesting graphs to help your data tell stories.

To get a quick visual of the shape of your data, you can import a library called matplotlib to help create charts and plot your data as a whole, as shown in Figure 10.8.

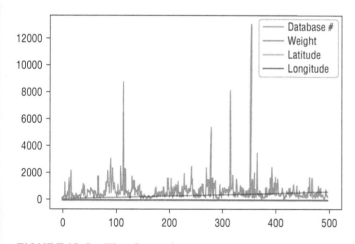

FIGURE 10.8: The first plot

To import the library and display the chart, enter the following code in the next cell of your notebook and again click the **Run** button:

```
import matplotlib.pyplot as plt
data.plot()
```

The first line of code pulls (imports) the matplotlib library into your project. The second plots or draws the data into the chart. Plotting your entire dataset doesn't tell you a great deal about the various aspects you want to focus on, so you need a bit more refinement in your plots.

What if you want to focus on the number of rocks that are available in this collection? Build a bar chart by entering the following code in a new cell and running it:

```
name = data.value_counts(data['Rock Name'].values, sort=True)
plt.rcParams['figure.figsize'] = [6, 12]
name.plot.barh()
```

In this code, you are able to specify that you want to get a count of the stones, sorted by Rock Name. Then, you want to see that count displayed in a bar chart that shows the Rock Name bars horizontally (barh) in a chart of 6 by 12 inches. The results of running this code are shown in Figure 10.9. It shows clearly (see Figure 10.9) that this dataset has a large quantity of quartzite, for example.

What if you wanted to learn the relationship between two elements within your data? For example, is there a relationship between the weight of a stone and its type? The following code creates a group of the data by Rock Name and gets the average (mean) of the weight of each type of stone. Then it plots a bar chart comparing the rocks by name to their average weights, as shown in Figure 10.10:

```
data = data.groupby('Rock Name').mean().reset_index()
rockWeight = data['Weight']
plt.barh(y=data['Rock Name'], width=rockWeight)
plt.rcParams['figure.figsize'] = [6, 12]
plt.show()
```

150

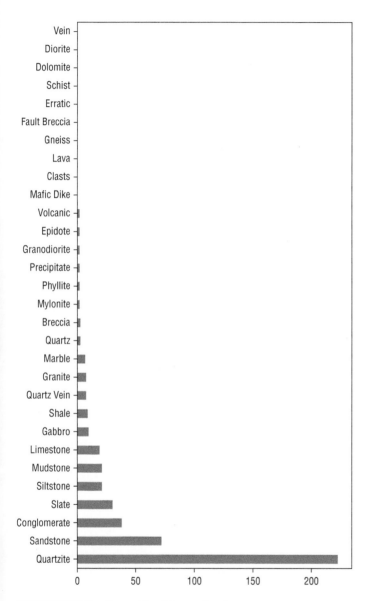

FIGURE 10.9: A vertical bar chart

151

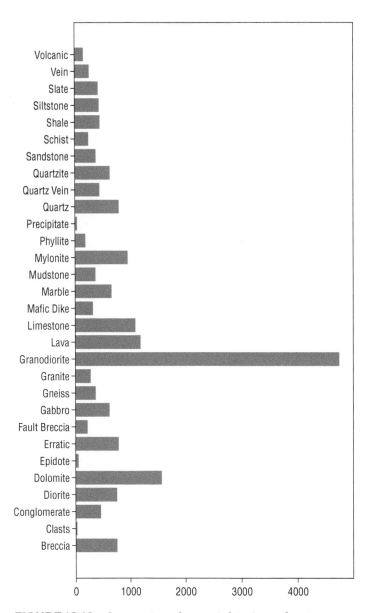

FIGURE 10.10: Averaging the weights in a chart

152

What has your data exploration told you about this dataset? In this case, you might start to think that the weight of a stone is dependent on its type— granodiorite seems like a really heavy stone. But perhaps it is just the particular samples that are heavy. Looking back at the original dataset, there are only two samples of this type of stone, and they are both very heavy. What's missing from this dataset is a measurement of the size (diameter or circumference) of the stone sample. You can see how your views of the data are shaped by the availability of various data points. In this case, there's an important missing piece!

Armed with this knowledge, you could return to your quantification of the stones in the riverbed and ensure that you gather all the data points you need, including the weight and size of a given stone sample as well as notes about color, texture, and shape. In this way, you could ensure that you would be able to make data-driven predictions—ideas based on an analysis of well-shaped data—about which of the stones in the creek might be geodes, which tend to be lighter in weight than their circumference might suggest.

Extend Your Knowledge

There are many different ways to clean data. Practice these skills by following the "Data Cleaning Challenge" on Kaggle found at `www.kaggle.com/code/rtatman/data-cleaning-challenge-handling-missing-values/notebook`.

Vocabulary Review

In your own words, describe:

- Data science
- Data visualization
- pandas

Quiz

Select the best answer for each of the following:

Q1: Why would you need to clean your data?
   a. Flawed data guarantees flawed results.
   b. Decisions made by analyzing data should be based on high-quality datasets.
   c. Both of these.

Q2: What type of errors might need to be removed from data you collect?
   a. Missing data
   b. Obsolete data
   c. Foreign data

Q3: What is data visualization used to do?
   a. Create memes
   b. Build GIFs and JPEGs
   c. Learn more about your data by looking at it as a visual artifact

Assignment: Data Tidy-Up

Making data usable for analysis is a critical part of data science. Practice transforming data to remove errors, highlighting or exposing relationships and making it more useful for analysis. Go to Kaggle and pick a dataset that you'd like to tidy up, as you practiced in this lesson. Pick four things to clean in your data and build a notebook on Kaggle that shows your work as you clean the data.

11. The Stone Library

Standard: 2-DA-09: Refine computational models based on the data they have generated

Now you know exactly what kind of data to collect, so you turn back to building your inventory of the rocks in the riverbed. The Guide looks over your shoulder at your growing collection of data and nods. "You're doing an excellent job of gathering information and organizing it," she says. "Now we know how many stones we have in this collection and which ones might be geodes."

Suddenly, you hear a strange noise. It sounds like a choked sort of scream, and you jump to your feet, startled. From the corner of your eye, you see a large black bird that has flown to a branch hanging over the creek. It points its large beak in your direction, fixes you with a quizzical stare, and yells "Caw!"

"Watch out!" shouts the Guide, as the bird launches itself into the air and starts flying directly toward you. You both jump back, expecting an attack. Instead, the crow veers straight to the collection of rocks and lands on a boulder in the creek. Cocking its head here and there, it selects a particularly knobby spherical stone and picks it up. You watch as it then flies to a high tree branch and drops the stone onto a large, flat rock. The stone breaks neatly in half and reveals its sparkling interior—the bird just stole a geode!

A second crow flies to the stone where the geode lies and is met by the first crow, who ceremoniously gives the other bird half the geode. They look at each other, pleased with their acquisition, pick up the geode parts, and fly merrily away.

The Guide smiles ruefully. "I forgot about the crows and thieving magpies. They love to acquire shiny, pretty objects—real collectors, they are—but really, we ought to find a way for them to borrow an object, enjoy it, and bring it back safely."

Puzzled, you think for a minute. Then you have it! "A sort of rock library?" you ask. "Exactly!" the Guide says happily. "I'm sure you can create something!"

Do Some Research

There are many ways that data are stored and shared, both on the web and between individual computers. So far, you have used a spreadsheet, probably stored in the cloud, to store your data. What if you wanted other people to have access to your data so that they could, effectively, make changes to your data in a secure manner? Buying an item from inventory, checking out a book, ordering a pizza, or saving a recipe are all tasks requiring users to access and update data.

Research the various ways that data can be stored and shared on the web. Check out different database systems such as MongoDB, MySQL, and PostgreSQL.

> **Note**
>
> There are some interesting differences between "relational" and "nonrelational" databases. Relational databases are structured with tables that have rows and columns, much like spreadsheets. Nonrelational databases are structured as documents, something like files. The ways in which a programmer queries, or extracts data from, these types of databases are quite different. In this chapter you'll explore relational databases.

Think Like a Computer Scientist

When it comes to storing data online or on a local server, several concerns are foremost in the mind of a computer scientist. Thinking at a systems level, a computer scientist or a database administrator (DBA) will be constantly thinking about ways to make the *querying* of data—the way the data is fetched from server to client—more performant and efficient.

One way databases can be made more performant is by using indexes. An index can be associated to a column in a table, such as a unique ID column. A copy

156

is made of this column and the values are stored in a separate table—an index table. When a query is made, the database can quickly look up the values in the index table and return the rows that match the query. As tables grow, querying them for data can become slower, so the use of indexes can help speed up querying.

Another big concern is security. Who has the right to access a database? What kind of data should be stored in a database? Consider the case of credit card numbers. It is a big security risk to store a full credit card number in a database, for fear of hacking. Increasingly, it's considered too risky to store sensitive information in a company's databases, so instead they outsource credit card storage and processing to a different company that specializes in secure storage.

> **Note**
>
> Research a particularly bad database security breach in recent years. How did the hackers access the data and what did they steal? Many countries have rules for the storage of personal information such as health care data. Look up your country's laws about these topics.

Finally, backing up databases, storing the backup in a safe place, and making sure that, in case of emergency, a database can be backed up and restored safely is a major concern. When a database's software needs to be upgraded, often that process brings with it the need to back up the current data and restore it.

Sketch It Out

Imagine you have two sets of data, the equivalent of two spreadsheets. One revolves around a collection of items; the other revolves around the people who interact with these items. A circulating library, for example, probably has a database listing all the items in their collection that people can check out using their library card. Think about what columns would be needed to keep track of the items. Then, think about how a person would go about borrowing one of these items. Ask yourself a few questions:

- Can every item be borrowed?
- Is every item available at the library?
- Is the item currently being borrowed?
- Is it necessary to track where the item is currently located?

Sketch out a database design for the collection items. It will look a lot like your spreadsheet of stones from the previous chapter.

Then, think about the borrower. How would people interact with your collection? Do you allow a family of multiple people to borrow an item using a shared card, or is each person required to have a card to borrow something? How do you keep track of who has borrowed what from the collection?

Sketch out a database design for the borrowers. You can make a few assumptions here:

- The borrower is a person.
- The borrower has a card.
- The borrower can borrow one or more items from the collection.
- The borrower can return any or all items to the collection.

Next, think about some "business logic" around a library. Do people have the right to borrow unlimited numbers of items, or must they return some before they can borrow others? What if they change their contact information? What if they lose an item? What if they want to borrow an item that is currently being borrowed?

Your sketch might look like Figure 11.1. You have a `users` table with a list of your users and a `cards` table that refers to a user's ID (called a `borrower_id` in the `cards` table). You also list your collection data in a `collection` table and display the history of the interactions between borrowers and collection items in the `collection_history` table.

158

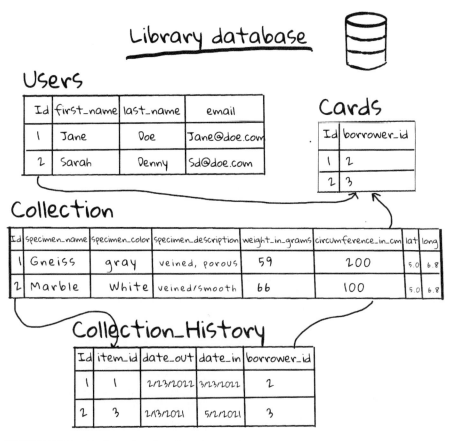

FIGURE 11.1: A sketch of a database design for a library

Your Challenge

Build a database that you can query given the business logic you have planned for your circulating rock library. It will consist of some tables with data. It should also include relationships between the tables.

Project Recipe

In this recipe you will use a handy browser tool called SQL Fiddle to learn how to design a database schema. You'll build part of the sketch you completed earlier with the goal of building the first elements of your rock library database.

> **Definition**
>
> A *schema* is a description of the database's structure.

Step 1: Build Your Collection Table

Go to `https://sqlfiddle.com` and choose the **SQLite (SQL.js)** option in the top drop-down, as shown in Figure 11.2. Click **Build Schema** to start.

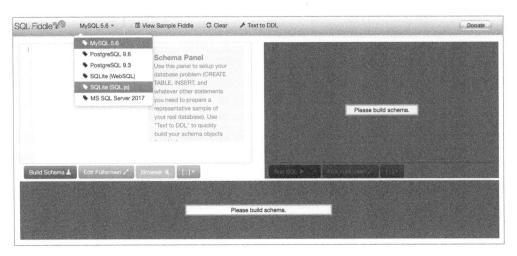

FIGURE 11.2: SQLITE in SQL Fiddle
Source: SQLFiddle.

Build your first table by using Structured Query Language (SQL). You can do so directly in the SQL Fiddle editor. Enter the following code into the panel on the left side of the screen:

```
CREATE TABLE collection (
    id INTEGER PRIMARY KEY AUTOINCREMENT,
    specimen_name TEXT,
    specimen_color TEXT,
    specimen_description TEXT,
    weight_in_grams INTEGER,
    circumference_in_cm INTEGER,
    lat INTEGER,
    long INTEGER);
```

Click **Build Schema** after adding this code. SQL Fiddle will execute the code, which creates your table, and then provide an alert that the schema is ready for use. The table that you created is called collection and includes several fields, which are like the columns of your spreadsheet table from Chapter 9, "Searching for Geodes."

The second line of the code creates the id field. The id field is an auto-incrementing integer primary key, which means it is a number that increments automatically as you add data so you never have to manually set a value for this type of field. It's a primary key, which means that it is a unique identifier for a row and can be used by other tables as a reference to look up given information.

The rest of the code creates the other fields in your collection table. The other fields also are delineated as text or integer, which helps shape your data as it is input into the table.

Step 2: Insert Data into the Collection

Now that you have your database table ready, it's time to insert some data. Add the following code under the Create Table code you added earlier in the left panel of SQL Fiddle:

```
INSERT INTO collection (specimen_name, specimen_color,
specimen_description, weight_in_grams, circumference_in_
cm, lat, long) VALUES ('Gneiss', 'gray', 'a mottled gray
rock', 100, 10, 37.8, -84.7);
```

This code adds one row of data to your table using an `INSERT` command. The new row will include all the fields about a given item in the collection except the `id`, which is added automatically. You can see that the code lists the names of the fields as well as the respective values for each field.

Add more rows to the table by copying this code and editing the data listed after `VALUES` to include other features of the rock collection. Maybe you can add some marble, granite, and basalt of different weights. Add the new `INSERT` statements below your current one. After entering the commands as shown in Figure 11.3, click the **Build Schema** button to add all four rows to your table.

```
SQL Fiddle

 1  CREATE TABLE collection (
 2      id INTEGER PRIMARY KEY AUTOINCREMENT,
 3      specimen_name TEXT,
 4      specimen_color TEXT,
 5      specimen_description TEXT,
 6      weight_in_grams INTEGER,
 7      circumference_in_cm INTEGER,
 8      lat INTEGER,
 9      long INTEGER);
10
11  INSERT INTO collection (specimen_name, specimen_color, specimen_description, weight_in_grams,
12                      circumference_in_cm, lat, long)
13                      VALUES ('Gneiss', 'gray', 'a mottled gray rock', 100, 10, 37.8, -84.7);
14  INSERT INTO collection (specimen_name, specimen_color, specimen_description, weight_in_grams,
15                      circumference_in_cm, lat, long)
16                      VALUES ('Marble', 'white', 'a veined white and gray rock', 120, 20, 37.6, -84.8);
17  INSERT INTO collection (specimen_name, specimen_color, specimen_description, weight_in_grams,
18                      circumference_in_cm, lat, long)
19                      VALUES ('Basalt', 'gray', 'a dark gray porous rock', 150, 40, 37.7, -84.5);
20  INSERT INTO collection (specimen_name, specimen_color, specimen_description, weight_in_grams,
21                      circumference_in_cm, lat, long)
22                      VALUES ('Puddingstone', 'red', 'a reddish veined rock', 500, 50, 37.9, -84.6);
```

FIGURE 11.3: Inserting data into your table
Source: SQLFiddle.

162

> **Tip**
>
> A shortcut to this task is allowed by SQL Fiddle. You can click the **Text to DDL** button and upload an exported copy of your spreadsheet from Chapter 9 as a CSV file if you're satisfied with the data.

Step 3: Query Your Data

Once you have your table built and the data imported, use the panel on the right to query it or extract the rows into a readable format. Do so by typing the following code into the Query panel on the right side of the SQL Fiddle workspace:

```
select * from collection
order by id asc
```

By using the `select *` keywords and specifying which table to target, you're requesting that SQL Fiddle fetch everything from your `collection` table. In addition, you asked that that data be ordered by ascending ID (lowest to highest). You should see the data you had inserted returned, as shown in Figure 11.4.

Congratulations! You just designed a basic database table and wrote your first SQL queries! Take some time to look through the code. You built a database table whose columns are designed to accept certain kinds of data, such as text or integers. Then, you populated the table with sample data in the matching format. Finally, you fetched all the data from that table using `select *`.

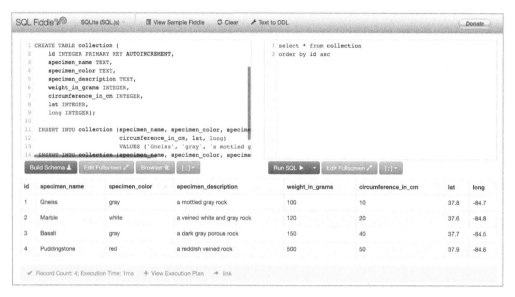

FIGURE 11.4: Querying your data
Source: SQLFiddle.

> **Note**
>
> This database, with just a few rows of data, is really small, so using the `select *` syntax, which selects everything in the table, is a good way to get started. When you want to make your queries more efficient, you can select individual columns by querying them by their unique IDs or by particular attributes, such as `where weight_in_grams = 100`.

Step 4: Create the *users* Table

Now, you need to think about how your collection might be used by the general public. Since you need to track who's borrowing an item, you must add

164

information about users to be stored in your database. Would you append data to your table as it stands or create a new table?

Since one user can potentially check out several items, you have a "one-to-many" logic to consider. You have to find a way to allow a given user to check out several items in your collection. Create a `users` table to store your users' data and connect it to your `collection` table. Do so by adding the following SQL code into the SQL Fiddle Schema panel under the other code already there:

```
CREATE TABLE users (id INTEGER PRIMARY KEY AUTOINCREMENT,
first_name TEXT, last_name TEXT, email TEXT);
INSERT INTO users (first_name, last_name, email) VALUES
('Sam', 'Smith', 'sam@smith.com');
```

This code creates a new `users` table with a primary key similar to that in the `collection` table. It also includes information about a user that would be useful for the library to know, such as their email address for communications and their first and last name.

Now you can query the users table as you did with your `collection` table earlier by typing a `select` statement in the Query panel:

```
select * from users
```

You should see `Sam Smith` as a user in the table. You can add some more users to the `users` table using the same technique you used to add items to the `collection` table.

Step 5: Connect Users to the Collection

Now you have two tables, which you can see by clicking **browser** in the Schema panel. Can you figure out how you can connect them? You have a couple of choices. You could create a lookup table to store the user ID and the collection ID so that one user could have several items checked out, one row per item.

A more efficient way would be to realize that one collection item can only be checked out by one user. So, if you associate that user's ID to the collection item, it will be understood that the user is in possession of that unique item.

165

Add a column to your `collection` table by editing the `Create Table Collection` statement at the top of the Schema panel. Put the following line after the creation of the collection table's ID field:

```
borrower_id INTEGER NULL
```

This will add a new field, `borrower_id`, with the option to allow it to remain empty, or null, if no borrower has yet claimed it. Whenever a borrower borrows an item, their ID can now be added to the `collection` table.

Edit the collection `INSERT` statements, adding a few existing user IDs from your `users` table to the new `borrower_id` field. If an item has not yet been checked out by a borrower, you can leave it as `null`. Your `collection` table `INSERT` SQL code now looks like the following:

```
INSERT INTO collection (specimen_name, borrower_id,
specimen_color, specimen_description, weight_in_grams,
circumference_in_cm, lat, long)
VALUES ('Gneiss', 1, 'gray', 'a mottled gray rock', 100,
10, 37.8, -84.7);
INSERT INTO collection (specimen_name, borrower_id,
specimen_color, specimen_description, weight_in_grams,
circumference_in_cm, lat, long)
VALUES ('Marble', 2, 'white', 'a veined white and gray
rock', 120, 20, 37.6, -84.8);
INSERT INTO collection (specimen_name, borrower_id,
specimen_color, specimen_description, weight_in_grams,
circumference_in_cm, lat, long)
VALUES ('Basalt', 3, 'gray', 'a dark gray porous rock',
150, 40, 37.7, -84.5);
INSERT INTO collection (specimen_name, borrower_id,
specimen_color, specimen_description, weight_in_grams,
circumference_in_cm, lat, long)
VALUES ('Puddingstone', null, 'red', 'a reddish veined
rock', 500, 50, 37.9, -84.6);
```

Now you can select the items that are currently being borrowed—in other words, where their `borrower_id` is not `null`—using the following line of code:

```
select specimen_name from collection WHERE borrower_id IS
NOT NULL
```

You now have the first few tables of a database that could eventually support a circulating rock library!

Step 6: Join Tables

Often, your queries need to show more complicated relationships, such as which items a given user has borrowed or which library members have requested a given item. In this case, you need to join some tables by connecting them via their keys. For example, if you wanted to build a query to show all the information about the user who has borrowed item 1, you would need to join the `users` and `collection` tables:

```
SELECT c.specimen_name, u.first_name, u.last_name
FROM collection c
JOIN users u ON u.id = c.borrower_id;
```

In this example, you have selected the fields you want to see from the `users` table. Then, you join the `collection` table to the `users` table by matching borrower IDs. By joining the `users` table to the `collection` table where the `borrower_id` column of the `collection` table is equal to the `id` column of the `users` table, you can see that the user has borrowed that item. You also use table aliases (like `c` for `collection` and `u` for `users`) to make the query more readable.

Extend Your Knowledge

Challenge yourself to make your database more detailed. Perhaps you want to show that a family shares a rock library card. How would you build another table to store all family members in one card? How would you increase the complexity of the table joins so that you can show all the members of a family who are associated with one item in a collection?

Read through the interesting types of joins and database queries you can make using SQLite by checking out its documentation: `https://sqlite.org/docs.html`.

Vocabulary Review

In your own words, describe:

- Business logic
- Field
- Join
- Query
- Schema
- SQL

Quiz

Select the best answer for each of the following:

Q1: You should never store personal information in a database.
  a. True
  b. False

Q2: You use SQL to query which of the following?
  a. Spreadsheet
  b. Relational database
  c. Nonrelational database

Q3: You index a database table to:
  a. Help with backups
  b. Make a database query run faster
  c. Copy data from one table to another

Assignment: Build Your Database

In this chapter, you built a model of a lending library by building its database schema, or design. The relationships between the tables mirror the relationships between objects and their borrowers. As a database grows, it might generate new relationships that you don't anticipate. Build a database design and explain how it might be used to generate new relationships.

An example might be a banking database, which might have a table of accounts and a table of transactions. Could you discover patterns of borrowing money that could lead to a marketing campaign or a new type of lending strategy?

Another example might be a museum, which would have a table of ticket sales linked to a table of exhibits. Could you discover patterns of people who are interested in an exhibit? How would you react to discovering such an insight?

12. Hide or Seek

Standard: 2-IC-23: Describe tradeoffs between allowing information to be public and keeping information private and secure

Now your database is built and populated with collections data. You start thinking about how to provide the forest residents with library cards if they would like to borrow a stone from the collection, perhaps using a handy birch bark square. The library is almost open for business and the Guide is very happy.

Looking around as the water courses musically over the stones, you notice a particularly large greenish boulder that you hadn't seen before, next to the collection. Did you forget to catalog it? Suddenly, you are startled as it starts to move! Very slowly, legs, a tail, and finally a head with ancient, wise eyes emerge from the domed object. You realize that, instead of a boulder, a large tortoise is looking around at the stream, blinking sleepily.

The Guide quickly approaches the tortoise. "Venerable friend, welcome! We hope we didn't disturb you." The tortoise shakes its head slowly, looking curiously at the piles of stones. "Would you be interested in acquiring the very first library card for our collection? I just need a little information from you and then I can register you in our system!" you chime in, excited about your first client. The tortoise smiles and reaches under its shell, pulling out a tattered note with its full address, Forest Security Number (FSN), contact information, snail mail address (actual snails deliver the mail in the forest, it seems), and more.

Dismayed, you look at all the information written down on the note. "I'm not sure I should know all this about you!" you say. The Guide nods and tells the tortoise kindly, "Let's find a better way to store your private information." The ancient tortoise, somewhat confused but willing to learn, agrees that there might be a better way than an old note full of personal details.

171

Do Some Research

Privacy, security, and compliance are key factors in the success of an organization. Even if they aren't particularly glamorous topics, there's nothing worse than a big privacy or security breach, so it's worth understanding the ramifications. In addition, keeping personal data private is increasingly difficult for individuals who might manage dozens of logins to various websites, including banks, shops, email, and social media sites.

> **Definition**
>
> In the context of Internet security, *compliance* refers to a business or government's rules to ensure that proper security protocols are followed.

In the previous chapter, you explored some implications for managing security for databases. Security involves how your personal information is protected — for example, in a bank with a well-architected database and website with proper login and password requirements.

Privacy, on the other hand, is all about your own personal information and how much of it you want to share publicly. For example, do you want to share your email address for anyone to see? How about your physical address? Should you share images of your baby sister's face, your government ID number, or how much money you have in the bank? How should you respond to Internet queries asking for this information?

Privacy and security often overlap. Security breaches can expose private data, for example. But it's important to understand the two domains as separate but complementary. One of the most important assets that is protected is called *personally identifiable information (PII)*. It's what allows an individual to be identified by something uniquely associated with them, such as a driver's license ID or passport number . It's what the old tortoise has written down on their tattered note — a note which, of course, can be lost or stolen.

> **Note**
>
> Visit the Department of Homeland Security's web page at `www`
> `.dhs.gov/privacy-training/what-personally-`
> `identifiable-information` for more information on security and privacy, including a useful video.

Research common ways that sensitive information is collected and shared on software systems. Take a look at some of the customizable privacy and security settings on various devices and software that can connect to the Internet.

> **Note**
>
> Older adults are particularly vulnerable to Internet scams, according to the FBI's annual report from 2021, found at `www.ic3.gov/Media/PDF/` `AnnualReport/2021_IC3Report.pdf`. Persons 60 and older lost the largest amount of money due to Internet scams—around $1.68 billion in 2021. They are susceptible to scams and loss because they often are less tech-savvy than their younger counterparts. They tend to be more trusting and have more financial assets than younger age groups, which makes them perfect targets for an online scammer. But regardless of your age, you will benefit from knowing more about how to protect yourself and your sensitive data.

Think Like a Computer Scientist

Where should the line be drawn between what is private and what is public in terms of shareable data? Often, that choice has legal consequences. Since computer scientists are often in charge of architecting systems, they need to have a clear grasp of the policies that govern the data that their systems collect and share. For this reason, websites usually have privacy policies. In fact, in California, it's the law! Take a look at the California Online Privacy Protection Act of 2003 (CalOPPA), which can be read at `https://consumercal.org/about-cfc/cfc-education-foundation/california-online-privacy-protection-act-caloppa-3`.

If you've visited European websites, you might have noticed the pop-ups that note that they use cookies to collect information about your visit to their site. That's due the European Union's General Data Protection Regulation (GDPR), which you can read about at `https://gdpr.eu`. GDPR requires that web sites reveal details about how they collect user information.

Software engineers need to understand the nature of the data they are handling and how to protect it. Visit `https://privacy101.org` and learn how various devices from mobile phones to web browsers to smart devices and wearables collect, store, and share data. Think about how you would build systems that are secure and private.

Your system may be compliant and secure and follow all the appropriate legal rules for keeping data safe. But a system is only as safe as the integrity of the person who has access to someone's personal information. Tricky techniques that target human weaknesses can cause users to help scammers bypass the best security systems. Take a look at three such techniques that scammers use:

Social Engineering When people are manipulated into giving up confidential information to a third party, that's called social engineering. Phone scams asking for passwords are a basic example. You might have also seen fraudulent emails apparently sent from trusted sources such as friends or family members. Other emails ask you to verify your personal information by clicking a fraudulent link that opens your system to scraping. A particularly nasty social engineering scam that directly targets elders is called the "grandparent scam," where the elder receives an email claiming that their grandchild is in danger and requests money.

Phishing Emails are another example of an attempt to fool the user into giving up personal information. During the Covid-19 pandemic, for example, emails have been sent from fraudulent addresses claiming to be legitimate pandemic information sources. Phishing emails appear to be legitimate, as they often are

174

designed to resemble a brand's email, but the content is fraudulent, as are any links in the email.

Spoofing   Like social engineering, spoofing uses legitimate-looking communications to trick people into clicking fraudulent links. Watch carefully for typos, false sender addresses, and off-brand links.

Sketch It Out

Hackers are always looking to gain access to people's lives and their sensitive information. They do this even while data is being collected about you, often without the knowledge of the person in question. Attackers are incentivized to trick people into revealing even more sensitive private information in order to gain access to their lives. Malicious Internet users leverage social engineering techniques, phishing, and spoofing to steal information, so let's examine these techniques and try to build a list of red flags to watch for so that someone like the old tortoise might be better able to keep their personal information safe.

Choose either social engineering, phishing, or spoofing and sketch a strategy to address such an attack. Imagine that your grandma, the tortoise, or another member of the forest stone library receives an email that appears to be from the stone library. The email is asking them to reset their login details, as the previous details have expired. What are the red flags that you can point to right away to encourage your elder friends not to click on suspicious links or buttons? Draw a scenario as a cartoon to show how such a conversation might go. Such a conversation with your grandma might look something like Figure 12.1.

175

FIGURE 12.1: A phishing email for Grandma

> **Note**
>
> There are several websites that offer free cartoon-strip software creation; `Canva.com` is good or you can try using `app.pixton.com`.

Your Challenge

As a computer scientist, you are responsible not only for building systems, but also for making them safe for all your users. Part of that work is the community-building educational work that helps inform users about malicious ways that bad actors spoof legitimate websites like yours in order to steal user credentials. Your challenge is to create a guide to help the vulnerable members of your community use your stone library's assets safely.

> **Note**
>
> If you don't have an easy way to connect with an older person in your family or community, create your guide for an adult you know or even a fellow student. Everyone is vulnerable to phishing and spoofing, so your work will be valuable for everyone!

Project Recipe

Because this chapter is about creating an asset to help your community, you won't be building a project for yourself. Rather, you'll be creating training materials to benefit a wider audience. Your job is to create a brief training video with a presentation outlining the ways that scammers try to play on older individuals' fears and weaknesses to gain access to their PII. Consider recording *alongside* an older individual to make a great presentation!

Step 1: Gather Evidence

Your first step is to understand the scams that are currently targeting older individuals. We mentioned phishing, spoofing, and social engineering earlier. At `https://ncoa.org/article/how-to-prevent-phishing-scams-a-guide-for-seniors`, the National Council on Aging (NCOA) lists several techniques that are used, including pleas for help, promises of having won a prize, threats to close accounts, or warnings that government agencies are closing in. All these techniques are designed to scare people reading this unsolicited email.

Research the red flags in this type of communication, such as misspellings, urgency, links that send a user to unknown sites, requests to reset passwords or to send Social Security information, and strange sender email addresses. Make a list of these red flags.

Gather examples of phishing emails and note the red flags from earlier. You can find examples at `https://us.norton.com/Internetsecurity-online-scams-phishing-email-examples.html`, or you might have ones of your own that you can screenshot—just don't click any links! You can use these in your presentation. Figure 12.2 presents a few very basic examples.

FIGURE 12.2: Sample phishing emails

Source: Microsoft Corporation.

178

Finally, ask your local police what they recommend older individuals do if they receive these types of fraudulent communications. The FBI has a reporting line at `www.ic3.gov`, but often the first line of defense is the local police. If your local police do not have a policy, consider working with them to help create one, including a place on their website for instructions on how to handle cyber-security problems.

Step 2: Build a Script

You should build a script for your training video based on what you gathered in Step 1. Target about five minutes of video that includes a slide presentation using Google Slides or another presentation program. Share your screen with images of scam emails, showing their red flags. Your script might have the following outline:

1. State the problem.
    i. Fraud is a big problem online.
    ii. Older individuals are particularly at risk.
    iii. There are some clear steps elders can take to educate themselves and protect themselves from fraud.
2. Give examples.
    i. Show a phishing email example and point out the red flags.
    ii. Do the same for a social engineering scheme.
    iii. End with an example of a spoofing email.
3. Role-play opening an email.
    i. Identify at least five red flags.
    ii. Give advice on what to do next, based on your research.

Step 3: Create Your Video

With your research complete and a script in hand, create your video. Use your phone or a laptop with a webcam to record. Consider recording with an older individual in the room to include them in the conversation. You can find good tips on setting up a film environment at `https://wistia.com/learn/production/shooting-video-by-yourself`.

Extend Your Knowledge

There are a myriad of privacy laws that have been introduced in response to the need to protect individuals online. Learn more on your own about the Gramm–Leach–Bliley Act (GLBA) governing banking and financial information, the Children's Online Privacy Protection Rule (COPPA), which governs the protection of children's data, the Health Insurance Portability and Accountability Act (HIPAA), various state laws, the General Data Protection Regulation (GDPR), and other privacy regulations. Make a timeline to understand how each of these were introduced at various moments during the Internet's evolution.

Vocabulary Review

In your own words, describe:

- Phishing
- PII
- Social engineering
- Spear phishing
- Spoofing

Quiz

Select the best answer for each of the following:

Q1: Phishing involves:
   a. Misdirected emails
   b. Emails from anonymous sources
   c. Emails from sources who are not who they say they are

Q2: PII stands for personally identifiable information.
   a. True
   b. False

Q3:   The GDPR allows for a user to:
a. Object to using their data for marketing purposes
b. Transfer their data from one system to another
c. Both of these

Assignment: A Training Manual

Now that you have a video instructional guide, work with an older individual in your community to help train them on how to protect themselves from phishing, spoofing, and social engineering attacks. Send them the video or watch it with them and ask for their feedback. Work with them to talk to their friends, perhaps in your local community center for older individuals. Get their thoughts on how to make your training manual more useful. With their feedback, add another element to your training guide, perhaps by building a small website, having your police department include your video on their website, or writing up a pamphlet, cartoon, or brochure to accentuate your training.

IV
The Petrified Forest

13. The Petrified Forest

Standards:

2-AP-10: Use flowcharts and/or pseudocode to address complex problems as algorithms

2-AP-16: Incorporate existing code, media, and libraries into original programs, and give attribution

The sun is hot overhead, and you feel tired. "Let's rest," says the Guide, sitting down in the shadow of a tall rock-like object. You are happy to comply, and after a few minutes, you lean against the shiny, crystal-like veined stone.

"Careful," warns the Guide, "it's fragile!"

You begin to observe your environment. You are surrounded by curious formations of fossilized wood that look like tree trunks that have been crystallized. Petrified wood is wood that has been turned into stone by a natural process called petrification. This part of the forest is hundreds of millions of years old! The Guide looks at the various rock formations and sighs. "This area is one of our most delicate parts of the forest," she reveals. Surprised, you wonder how such solid stones could be in danger.

"While most of our forest residents mean no harm, sometimes the more . . . blundering types . . . bump up against these formations and crack them, tip them over, or damage them. They mean no harm, but the stones, while strong, are actually quite brittle," says the Guide, frowning. "I would love to find a natural way to warn the residents that they're entering a fragile area that could be damaged. Could you help us? We might have to enlist the cooperation of some of our more lightweight citizens."

You'll need to find a way to map the terrain of this part of the forest and, by observing their behavior, determine which animals might unintentionally damage the wood formations versus those who might be able to act as defenders.

185

Do Some Research

Your task, according to the Guide, is to build a map of this part of the forest, with all its strange formations, and to give the Guide an idea of the potential for damage from those who visit it. Essentially, you're building a model for the Guide that will provide suggestions for how to react to patterns of behavior. Friend or potential problem? How can such judgments be made?

Consider a national park, where the staff needs to understand which visitors might want to spend the night camping inside the park. What behaviors might trigger a park ranger's suggestion to reserve a campground ahead of time?

Sketch It Out

Think of the information that will help you to understand who should have access to the forest grove and who shouldn't. Create a flowchart of "friend" and "enemy" behaviors that might alert an administrator about visitors' intentions. Your flowchart might resemble Figure 13.1.

Note

A *flowchart* is a visual representation of a decision-making process, including inputs, questions, answers, and outputs. There is a specific visual vocabulary used to create flowcharts that can be seen at `https://asq.org/quality-resources/flowchart`. You can create a flowchart using free software online, such as Google Drawings. To create a flowchart in Google Drawings, create a Google account if you don't yet have one (ask your parent, teacher, or guardian for help if needed) and navigate to `https://docs.google.com/drawings`. Use the shape icon in the navigation bar to select shapes to add to your workspace. Edit the shapes, colors, and labels of your flowchart to your preference.

While you are working through your charting tasks, consider the side consequences of this type of user profiling. How can poor decisions be made based on biased information? How can this type of profiling impact the real world and the people in it?

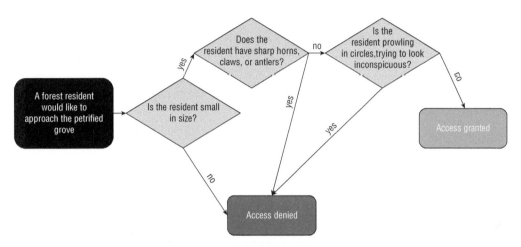

FIGURE 13.1: A flowchart for forest visitors created using the free online tools at Google Drawings

Think Like a Computer Scientist

By taking many inputs and progressing through a series of steps, computer scientists build up algorithms that can be used to make decisions. Algorithms are a very old mathematical concept named after the ninth-century Persian mathematician Muḥammad ibn Mūsā al-Khwārizmī. Algorithms are a way of thinking about a problem in terms of a set of instructions.

Algorithms are all around us, not just in obscure math problems. Do you have a method to sort the many pairs of mismatched socks once they exit the dryer? One way would be to pick one sock and then sort through an entire pile of socks to find its match. That's not very efficient. It's called *naïve searching* and takes a long time to match just one sock. A better strategy would be to sort the socks by color, then sort those piles by size, and finally by pattern. Eventually you have small enough piles to easily make matches. Each of these techniques is called a *sort algorithm*. Where else would you use a sort algorithm?

187

Algorithms are used for building decision-making models such as the one you are sketching. In the context of retail, an algorithm could be constructed that watches a customer interacting with a storefront and gathers data about purchasing habits, likes, and avoidances. Then, an algorithm can be used to recommend items to the customer based on the data gathered. In the context of the petrified forest, you are building a system to predict user intent by observing their behavior.

Your Challenge

Your challenge is to build a world model of the petrified forest and prepare to populate it with characters who will interact with one another. To do this, you'll work in 3D! A-Frame is a web framework for building 3D virtual reality experiences right in the browser. With it, you can create all kinds of interesting worlds. In the process, you can also use code developed by others, but it's important to respect the original creator's preferences as to exactly how to reuse their work. You want to be sure to give correct attribution and pay attention to licenses, which give important details about how code can be used.

Let's build a virtual forest! This forest will have a benign friend who will hover over the grove without touching it, and a potential enemy, a cat. This cat prowls around somewhat menacingly and is armed with sharp claws that could damage the wood, as you described in your flowchart.

Project Recipe

To get started with A-Frame, you need a modern browser such as Chrome, Edge, or Firefox with an Internet connection. You also need a way to build a 3D world in a publishable format. For this project you can use Glitch (found at `https://glitch.com`) as a development environment.

Step 1: Create an Account and Starter Project

Create an account on Glitch to save your work. Once your account is created, go to the A-Frame starter project, which can be found at `https://glitch.com/~aframe`. Copy (or, in Glitch's terminology, "Remix"), and copy it to your Glitch account by clicking the **Remix your own** button, which you can see in the lower-right corner of the page, as seen in Figure 13.2.

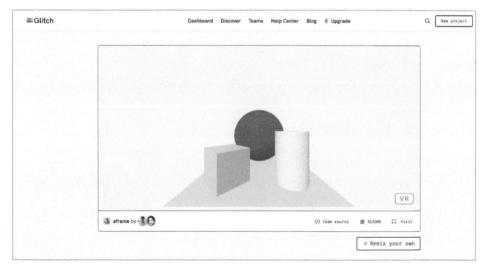

FIGURE 13.2: An A-Frame starter project on Glitch
Source: Glitch.

189

After clicking the button to copy this project to your own account, click **index .html** in the left navigation and then **preview** ➤ **open preview pane** at the bottom. You'll see a basic 3D view of a cylinder, cube, and sphere, as shown in Figure 13.3. Notice that you can click and drag the scene on the right-hand screen in Glitch to view it from different angles.

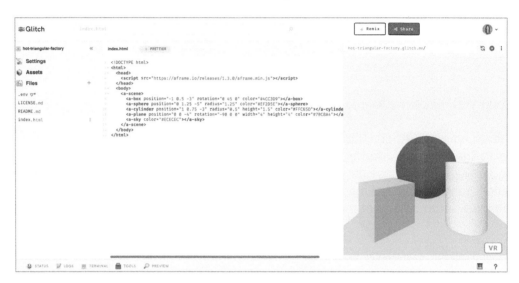

FIGURE 13.3: The A-Frame interface

Source: glitch.

Step 2: Observe the HTML Tags

By editing the HTML markup in the `index.html` file, you can lay out a new world! HTML is Hypertext Markup Language, a markup language that allows you to create web pages using tags, the building blocks of HTML. Normally you'll find HTML in an `index.html` file. A-Frame has special HTML tags that you can use to build a 3D world.

190

Looking at the information in the `index.html` file shown in Figure 13.3, you should notice how the HTML tags are laid out to create this scene. The `<body>` tag is the root of the scene, and the other tags are for things like the sky, the floor, and the items on the plane.

The items are stacked in the HTML as they are stacked in this virtual world. The box, sphere, and cylinder are set on top of the plane, which is on top of the background, or "sky." Just as you paint a painting, you layer the elements as you'd like them to appear in the virtual world.

Try editing the HTML tags to become more familiar with this interface. Change the first `<a-box>` tag to change the cube's color to hot pink: `<a-box position="-1 0.5 -3" rotation="0 45 0" color="#DF00FF"></a-box>`. Once you are comfortable with the Glitch interface, you can start building your world.

Step 3: Add External Libraries

A-Frame is primarily built using HTML and JavaScript. To create a scene, you will start by using just HTML.

Working in the index.html file in your Glitch workspace, start building your world by adding tags. Looking at the code in the index.html file, which you can see in the left pane of Figure 13.3, you'll see there is a header section that starts with <head> and ends with </head>. This area is where you'll add the files that power your A-Frame world. The A-Frame script seen in Figure 13.3 is importing the A-Frame library using a script tag, but for your new world scene, you need to import two more external libraries. Replace the entire <head> tag section within your index.html file with the following markup:

```
<head>
    <title>A Forest</title>
    <meta name="description" content="A Forest" />
    <script src="https://aframe.io/releases/1.0.0/aframe.
min.js"></script>
    <script src="https://unpkg.com/aframe-environment-
component@1.1.0/dist/aframe-environment-component.min.
js"></script>
    <script src="https://cdn.rawgit.com/donmccurdy/aframe-
extras/v5.0.0/dist/aframe-extras.min.js"></script>
</head>
```

In this new HTML markup, a title and description have been added for your world along with three scripts:

- The aframe.io library, imported from the A-Frame website
- The aframe-environment-component library, used when you want to add special components to your world
- An "extras" library that is necessary for adding animated characters to your world

192

Step 4: Build the Main Scene

Now you can start building the `<body>` tag of your document. While the `<head>` area of your HTML page includes files and tags that set up your scene, including things like its description and the page title, the bulk of your HTML that is seen in the browser is built in the `<body>` tag.

Remove the elements currently inhabiting the body tag (all the items between `<body>` and `</body>` in the code shown in Figure 13.3). Start by adding a scene to the body using the following code:

```
<body>
    <a-scene>
    </a-scene>
</body>
```

This code will form the basis of your A-Frame scene. You'll start adding tags into the scene as you build your forest.

Step 5: Populate the Forest

Populate your scene with a forest by adding an entity. In A-Frame, an *entity* is a placeholder that can be given attributes such as geometry, material, or a light source. Learn more about entities at `https://aframe.io/docs/1.3.0/core/entity.html`. Add the following code between the `<a-scene>` tags to add a preconfigured forest scene:

```
<a-entity environment="preset:forest"></a-entity>
```

A-Frame's component library comes with preset scenes you can use, and this scene works well for your forest. Your scene should now contain a forest that looks similar to Figure 13.4. Explore the forest scene by using your mouse to drag the screen around.

FIGURE 13.4: The forest scene

Source: glitch.

Step 6: Add Petrified Wood

Now, add petrified wood. You can use cylinders such as the one in Figure 13.3 to emulate the wood. Add the following code after the close of the `</a-entity>` tag:

```
<a-cylinder src="https://raw.githubusercontent.com/
CS4Kids/sketchfab-models/main/images/wood.jpg" position="1
0.75 -3" radius="0.25" height="0.5"></a-cylinder>
<a-cylinder src="https://raw.githubusercontent.com/
CS4Kids/sketchfab-models/main/images/wood.jpg" position="1
0.75 -2" radius="0.090" height="1.5"></a-cylinder>
<a-cylinder src="https://raw.githubusercontent.com/
CS4Kids/sketchfab-models/main/images/wood.jpg" position="1
0.75 -1" radius="0.15" height="1.35"></a-cylinder>
<a-cylinder src="https://raw.githubusercontent.com/
CS4Kids/sketchfab-models/main/images/wood.jpg" position="2
0.75 -1" radius="0.35" height="1.25"></a-cylinder>
```

194

```
<a-cylinder src="https://raw.githubusercontent.com/
CS4Kids/sketchfab-models/main/images/wood.jpg" position="3
0.85 -1.5" radius="0.15" height="1.25"></a-cylinder>
```

This code creates five cylinders of various sizes within the scene and uses a wood image (`wood.jpg`) to color them. You can position the cylinders as you like by editing the `position` parameter of this tag. The three position numbers refer to the x, y, and z coordinates (also known as width, height, and depth) in a three-dimensional space.

Customize your forest by changing the position, radius, and height of the cylinders. Add more petrified trees (cylinders) if you like!

> **Note**
>
> You are using a wood background image that is hosted in this book's GitHub repo, an image created by the author of this book. You can substitute other textures if you want, but be careful to use only free and open-license images. Creative Commons licenses are best for our purposes. Take a few minutes to visit some other GitHub repositories to see what kind of licenses are included with the software.

Step 7: Add Characters

Now, experiment with populating your forest with some characters. Included in this book's GitHub repo (`https://github.com/CS4Kids/graphic-assets`) are a rhino, two butterflies, a cat, and a hummingbird. You can place one, or all of them, in the forest by adding an `<a-assets>` section under the cylinder tags. In the `<a-assets>` tag, you will add one `<a-asset-item>` per animal. You will also add an `<a-entity>` for each animal. The asset item tag imports the model that will be used in the scene. In this case, the model is an animation imported from Sketchfab (`https://sketchfab.com`), which is an

195

online library where you can find free 3D assets to use in your virtual reality worlds and games.

Enter the following code after the final cylinder asset to add characters to your scene. In Glitch's interface, you can click **prettier** to tidy up the code so it will be well formatted:

```
<a-assets>
<!--This work is based on "Bengal" (https://sketchfab.
com/3d-models/bengal-8ad92b45ee7e4310b65669d3750a3313)
by ann55010970637 (https://sketchfab.com/ann55010970637)
licensed under CC-BY-4.0 (http://creativecommons.org/
licenses/by/4.0/)-->

<a-asset-item id="cat-model" src="https://raw.githubuser-
content.com/CS4Kids/sketchfab-models/main/bengal/scene.
gltf" crossorigin="anonymous"></a-asset-item>

<!--This work is based on "Borboleta Azul - Butterfly"
(https://sketchfab.com/3d-models/borboleta-azul-butterfly-
ab9192b6bc8f49e3baed63e984c7073a) by Lancaster Modelagem
3D (https://sketchfab.com/lancastermodelagem3d) licensed
under CC-BY-4.0 (http://creativecommons.org/licenses/
by/4.0/)-->

<a-asset-item id="butterfly-model" src="https://raw.
githubusercontent.com/CS4Kids/sketchfab-models/main/blue-
butterfly/scene.gltf" crossorigin="anonymous"></a-asset-
item>
</a-assets>

<a-entity id="cat" scale="1.5 1.5 1.5" position="-.5 1 -2"
gltf-model="#cat-model" animation-mixer></a-entity>
```

```
<a-entity id="butterfly" scale="1 1 1" position="1
1.53 -2" gltf-model="#butterfly-model" animation-
mixer></a-entity>
```

In this code you'll find statements surrounded by `<!--` and `-->` elements. These are code comments, and they are not displayed on the page but allow developers and anyone viewing code sources to see notes from the developer. It's good practice to give an attribution of your Sketchfab model right in the code as in the earlier example. Note the code comments that state the Sketchfab model's author, source, and license.

Nice! Now you have a butterfly fluttering in your forest and a Bengal cat prowling around similar to what is shown in Figure 13.5. Experiment with other creatures from the CS4Kids GitHub repo (`https://github.com/CS4Kids/graphic-assets`). Don't forget to add the attribution giving credit to the artist by adding a comment to the code.

FIGURE 13.5: The forest scene with animated animals
Source: glitch.

197

Extend Your Knowledge

As mentioned earlier, A-Frame is a library that uses HTML and JavaScript to create 3D virtual worlds. It is a lot like building a website because you use the same skills to work in this 3D world as you would building on the web. Like any good programmer, you probably want to read documentation about this new library that you're learning. Take time to read through the documentation at `https://aframe.io` and to walk through A-Frame School (`https://aframe.io/aframe-school`) for a tutorial on building Web VR interfaces.

As you work with A-Frame, you will be using a variety of tools from other libraries, including free, freemium (a model that eventually charges for some parts of its platform), and open source. A-Frame and Glitch are free platforms, with some paid services. In your code, you import the A-Frame library via a content delivery network (CDN), which is designed for fast delivery of assets for your apps. While you don't have to cite the source of your CDN-delivered libraries (although you can in your code comments), you should cite the source of code snippets, assets, or samples that you incorporate into your apps.

Vocabulary Review

In your own words, describe:

- A-Frame
- Algorithm
- CDN
- Creative Commons license
- Flowchart
- 3D

Quiz

Select the best answer for each of the following:

Q1: You use A-Frame to build this type of scene on the web:
   a. 1D
   b. 2D
   c. 3D

Q2: A CDN is used to:
   a. Cause audio to play in your apps
   b. Enhance security in your apps
   c. Import external assets into your applications

Q3: A flowchart can be described as:
   a. A chart that shows all the elements of an application
   b. A way to describe the flow of an application
   c. A visualization of decision-making processes

Assignment: Pave the Way

Modify the flowchart you created earlier to add more types of behaviors that might enable or disable access to a protected area. It's your world, so you can change how you want it to work!

Think about the creatures who might inhabit this world and decide whether they might be classified as friend or enemy. How will you know? What patterns will you observe in their behavior to determine their objective? Which ones will protect the petrified wood, and which will try to steal it or inadvertently damage it? Build a flowchart to map out the behaviors of several types of protectors and several potential marauders. You probably guessed it, but your next steps will be to build a game within this world to protect the forest from invaders.

14. The Butterfly Brigade

Standard: 2-AP-11: Create clearly named variables that represent different data types and perform operations on their values

Your model of the forest populated by creatures is coming along well. Looking up from your work, you notice movement out of the corner of your eye. Hearing twigs snap and a strange grunting, you turn to the Guide, who is looking in the direction of the noise apprehensively.

"Sounds like the wild boars that wander around this area," she says. "Let's retreat behind this tree and watch what happens. You don't really want to tangle with them!"

Along with the Guide, you scramble behind a large tree and peep out. A family of wild boars trots into the clearing where the petrified wood is, rooting around the trunks of the crystallized formations, grunting when they don't find the acorns they are searching for. Using their tusks, they plow up the turf for a while, searching for food.

Suddenly, you hear a strange whirring and, looking up, you discover a surprising sight. A flock of butterflies is headed toward the grove of petrified wood.

"Hooray!" cheers the Guide, peering out from behind the tree, "The butterfly brigade is here!"

You watch, astonished, as the butterflies encircle the grove of petrified wood and flutter their wings all together in the direction of the boars. Shocked, you watch the boars meander off, effectively shooed away by the army of butterflies. "How on Earth did that happen?" you ask, not quite believing your eyes.

"It's one of the mysteries of life," said the Guide, "the butterfly effect, when small changes can have big consequences." It certainly seems to have worked here, and you wonder whether you could re-create the effect to form a protective barrier around the fragile trees.

Your Challenge

Your challenge in this section is to enhance your 3D world with a bit of magic. You need to refactor your code so that each tree in your petrified forest has a number of butterflies to protect it. You'll enhance your code by refactoring some of it from HTML tags into JavaScript so that you'll have more control over how many trees you place in your grove and how many butterflies surround the petrified grove.

Sketch It Out

Sketch out a vision of how your world might look with a prowling enemy approaching butterflies hovering over the petrified grove. Your sketch might resemble Figure 14.1.

FIGURE 14.1: Sketching your A-Frame project

Think Like a Computer Scientist

In the previous chapter, you learned how A-Frame uses HTML to place elements in a 3D world. In plain HTML, it's not straightforward to dynamically spawn, or generate, new characters onto a screen. For this, you need to turn to a scripting language such as JavaScript. Fortunately, A-Frame uses browser technologies to display 3D worlds. You're going to use an important aspect of browser technology, the Document Object Model (DOM), to add elements to your world.

> **Note**
>
> The DOM represents a web page and its elements in a computer's memory as a tree-like structure that can be used by browsers to add elements to a screen. The DOM is built of several application programming interfaces (APIs) that allow programmers to identify parts of a web page on which to build elements. Read more about the DOM on the Mozilla Developer Network at `https://developer.mozilla.org/docs/Web/API/Document_Object_Model`.

For example, a block of text could be surrounded by a `<p>` tag in HTML. This indicates that the block is a paragraph of text, and it can be referenced by a programmer using the DOM's document interface:

`document.getElementsByTagName('p').`

A way to locate a specific element in a DOM tree is finding it by its unique reference, an attribute called `id`. If the tag has such an `id`(`<p id='myParagraph'>`), the specific paragraph in question could be accessed and manipulated by a programmer in a different way, such as:

`document.getElementById('myParagraph')`

Thus, accessing the DOM elements allows a programmer to have a lot of control over the appearance and functionality of a web page when pairing JavaScript with HTML. In the project recipe in this chapter, you will refactor your HTML code to build your 3D world in part using JavaScript.

> **Definition**
>
> *Refactoring* is a methodical rewriting of code to make it easier to read, more performant, and better written in general.

To make changes to the DOM using JavaScript, you're going to need to use variables. You already used variables in earlier chapters when building your games using MakeCode. As you may remember, variables can hold values that you can refer to in your code. In this chapter, you're going to create variables directly in JavaScript, paying attention to their names (to ensure sound naming practices for readability) and how they are used in the application.

JavaScript is an extremely forgiving language that allows a developer to choose almost any name for functions and variables. This flexibility puts the burden on you or your team to decide the best naming pattern, or naming convention, for the elements in your projects. JavaScript does respect case sensitivity, so a variable named `MyVar` is not the same as a variable named `myVar`. Other than that, there are just a few general rules to remember:

- Name your variables and functions in a way that explains what they do or what they represent.
- Use camel case for naming both functions and variables. Using this convention, the first letter of the name is not capitalized but remaining words are, like the humps on a camel: `getFirstName` and `cityOfResidence` are examples.
- When writing a function, use a verb as the first part of its name, like `getRandomElements` or `saveToFile`.
- Constants, which are special kinds of variables, are written in uppercase, as described later in this chapter.
- Booleans, which you have used before, are usually prefixed with `is`, `are`, or `has`, such as `isValid` or `hasMultipleValues`.

204

Project Recipe

In this recipe, you'll enhance the previous version of your A-Frame project. You will replace repetitive code, use additional files to organize your project, and update your world to use JavaScript to dynamically add trees and butterflies.

Step 1: Copy Your Previous World

Go to the first version of your forest in Glitch and click **Remix** at the top to create a new copy. This copy will be named something random like **stingy-beryl-wholesaler.glitch.me**. You can change its name by clicking the **Settings** button in the left navigation and then selecting **Edit project details** to display the dialog box shown in Figure 14.2.

> ### Note
>
> You can find clean copies of the finished code for each chapter at `https://cs4kids.club/kids` if you need it.

You can change the project's name, enter a description, and then click **Save**. Now you're ready to start refactoring your HTML and to make the layout of your world more dynamic using JavaScript.

Step 2: Remove Repetitive Code

If you observe the HTML that's already in your `index.html` file, you might notice that you are violating an important principle of software development: "don't repeat yourself," or DRY. The forest, in fact, is laid out with many repeated HTML tags. For example, `<a-cylinder>` is repeated five times with only a few modifications around the position, radius, and height. Not only is this code repetitive, but it's also not dynamic. The position, radius, and height elements are hard-coded to fixed values and aren't easy to change. You can make the

205

screen layout more flexible for future edits by laying out the grove dynamically using code.

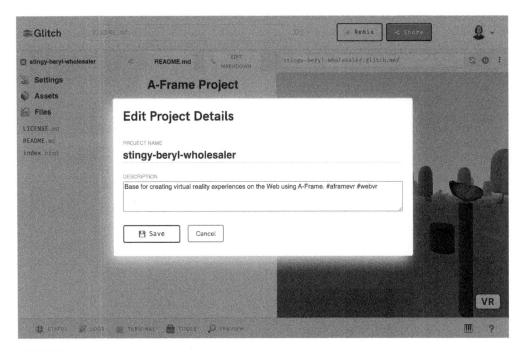

FIGURE 14.2: Renaming your A-Frame project

Source: Microsoft Corporation.

Delete all the `<a-cylinder>` tags from `index.html` by highlighting their code and pressing Delete.

Step 3: Create a Random Number Function to Create New Cylinders

You're now going to create two functions and then a loop to lay out a series of cylinders by leveraging the DOM's ability to add elements to HTML by using JavaScript. These will be placed in a new file, which you can create and add to your project by clicking the blue **+** button to the right of the Files menu option

206

located in the left panel in Glitch. In the resulting dialog box, enter the new file named **grove.js** and then click **Add This File** to add grove.js to your workspace.

With the new file added, you can create a function called **getNum** at the top of the grove.js file by adding the following code:

```
function getNum(minNum, maxNum) {
   return Math.random() * (maxNum - minNum) + minNum;
}
```

In this code, you're fetching a number generated by passing in a minimum and a maximum value. Notice that you named your function so that it's clear what will happen, and you pass in variables that designate the type of data and its nature: minNum and maxNum. You're also using JavaScript's built-in Math.random() function that generates a number that is no lower than the first number passed in (and might equal it). The generated number also won't be greater than the second number passed in, a maximum value.

Step 4: Create the Grove of Trees Dynamically

You can use the getNum() function you just created by adding a createTree() function. This function re-creates the HTML that you just removed from the index.html file in Step 2 but uses JavaScript to generate the trees. Add the following code after the getNum() function's code in your grove.js file:

```
function createTree() {
   let cylinder = document.createElement("a-cylinder");
   cylinder.setAttribute(
      "src",
      "https://raw.githubusercontent.com/CS4Kids/
sketchfab-models/main/images/wood.jpg"
   );
   cylinder.setAttribute("position", {x: getNum(1,3), y: 0,
z: getNum(-1,-2)});
```

```
cylinder.setAttribute("radius", getNum(0,0.5));
cylinder.setAttribute("height", getNum(0,2));
document.querySelector("a-scene").appendChild(cylinder);
}
```

In this function, you are creating tree-like cylinder elements and appending them to the `<a-scene>` element laid out in the HTML. You also used `setAttribute` to add attributes to your grove, including using the `getNum()` function to generate position, radius, and height randomly. Now, you have less control over the exact position, height, and radius of your trees' placement, but you still have some constraints over the general area, radius, and height of your grove.

You probably noticed that nothing has appeared yet on your screen. That's partly because you haven't yet called the function you just created. Call the `createTree` function by adding a loop at the bottom of your `grove.js` file that calls your function within the loop:

```
for (let index = 0; index < 5; index++) {
  createTree()
}
```

This loop states that, for a variable called `index` that is incremented each time the loop runs as long as its value is less than 5, run the function `createTrees`.

The last step to build your grove is to add a reference to `grove.js` into the HTML at the bottom of the `index.html` file. This added reference will allow the code to run after the scene is built. Add the following line of code to the bottom of your `index.html` file, just above the `</body>` tag:

```
<script src="grove.js"></script>
```

Your screen should display a world that looks similar to Figure 14.3. Because of the use of the random function `getNum`, your petrified trees will be located in different places in your world! In fact, run this program again and you will notice that the trees show up in new locations.

FIGURE 14.3: A dynamically built grove
Source: Microsoft Corporation.

Step 5: Change the View with a Camera

You have probably noticed that your view of the world is rather close up. A camera can be added to better control the view that you have of your environment. Add a camera by adding the following code right under the first `<a-entity>` tag:

```
<a-entity camera position="0 3 5" look-controls>
</a-entity>
```

Adding a camera gives you a wider view of the scene and better control over the experience. You can read more about the camera in the A-Frame documentation found at `https://aframe.io/docs/1.3.0/components/camera.html`.

> **Note**
>
> Notice that the camera position takes three parameters. These refer to the x, y, and z coordinates of a 3D space.

Step 6: Build Butterflies Dynamically

Just as you did for the grove, you can build dynamically generated butterflies to further reduce your hard-coded HTML code and make a more interesting world. Add a file called **butterflies.js** in the same way you added grove.js.

Before building a dynamic group of butterflies, delete the existing HTML for the butterfly entity from the index.html file:

```
<a-entity
      id="butterfly"
      scale="1 1 1"
      position="1 1.53 -2"
      gltf-model="#butterfly-model"
      animation-mixer
    ></a-entity>
```

Since you're going to use the same sort of number generation technique as you used in the grove, you can delete the getNum() function from grove.js and move it to index.html. Add the following code just above the closing </head> tag in index.html:

```
function getNum(minNum, maxNum) {
  return Math.random() * (maxNum - minNum) + minNum;
}
```

Now you can build the butterfly group. Add the following code to the `butterflies.js` file you created. This will generate 10 butterflies hovering over the grove:

```
function createButterfly() {
  let butterfly = document.createElement("a-entity");
  butterfly.setAttribute("gltf-model", "#butterfly-model");
  butterfly.setAttribute("position", "0 1 -2");
  butterfly.setAttribute("position", {
    x: getNum(1, 2),
    y: getNum(1, 2),
    z: getNum(0, -2),
  });
  butterfly.setAttribute("animation-mixer", "timeScale:
1");
  document.querySelector("a-scene").appendChild(butterfly);
}

for (let index = 0; index < 10; index++) {
  createButterfly();
}
```

Add the script to the bottom of the `index.html` file under the `grove.js` script by adding the following:

```
<script src="butterflies.js"></script>
```

Your world should now look like Figure 14.4.

FIGURE 14.4: A world with a grove and butterflies

Source: Microsoft Corporation.

Step 7: Control the Numbers of Trees with a Constant

There is one more edit you can make to your code to give yourself even more control over the dynamic nature of this world. Create a constant or a variable that can be used throughout the files of your program and that will need to be edited in one place if necessary. In the script block in the `index.html` file, above the `getNum()` function add the following code:

```
const NUM_TREES = 5;
```

Now, you can use this value throughout and edit it to change the nature of your world, if you like. Edit the `for` loop in `grove.js` to use this constant:

```
for (let index = 0; index < NUM_TREES; index++) {
  createTree();
}
```

212

Then, edit the `for` loop in `butterflies.js` to allow three butterflies to be generated per tree:

```
for (let index = 0; index < NUM_TREES*3; index++) {
  createButterfly();
}
```

You now have a very respectable array of butterflies hovering over the grove, flapping their wings! Experiment with different numbers of trees to see the best number of elements for your own world. How does it look if there are 20 trees?

Extend Your Knowledge

Naming conventions for variables and functions differ by language. Do a little research to learn more about how Java, PHP, Swift, Go, and other languages specify naming things. Why do you think some languages have different conventions than others?

Vocabulary Review

In your own words, describe:

- Constant
- DOM
- DRY

Quiz

Select the best answer for each of the following:

Q1: Variables should be named so that:
   a. They are easier to use in code
   b. It's easy to understand what they refer to
   c. They can be more easily used in functions

Q2: DRY in software development refers to:
   a. Don't cause infinite loops
   b. Don't repeat yourself when writing code
   c. Don't write random variable names
Q3: In JavaScript, constant names are most often written in:
   a. Camel case
   b. Uppercase
   c. Lowercase

Assignment: Code Hunt

In this chapter, you worked to refactor your code and make it more DRY. Go back over other assignments from this book, from a different coding project, or even from someone else's code on GitHub, and improve it. Use the techniques you learned in this chapter to rename variables and functions according to best practices and refactor the code to avoid repetition. Present a "before and after" view of your work using the worksheet provided on the CS4Kids website at `https://cs4kids.club/assets/ch14-worksheet.pdf`.

15. Power of the Weak

Standards: 2-AP-12: Design and iteratively develop programs that combine control structures, including nested loops and compound conditionals

You watch as the collective breeze from the butterfly wings and the flashing colors produced by their fluttering effectively repel the boar family, who amble off, grunting discontentedly, back into the forest. You can even feel the draft ruffle your hair. Small as they are, together the butterflies wield surprising force! The Guide breathes a sigh of relief as the butterflies slow their flapping wings and start to disperse.

"I feel like the real drama of that scene isn't quite captured in your current model," says the Guide, coming out from behind the tree. "What if you could make the world behave more like it does in the forest, where prowlers are repelled by the butterflies?"

You think this might be possible, but you'll need to incorporate some more elements into your environment, notably a physics engine that can handle collisions so that if a prowler approaches the petrified wood too closely, it is repelled by the fluttering butterfly battalion. It seems like an interesting challenge, so you get to work.

Do Some Research

Most games and many virtual worlds incorporate "physics libraries," which help handle collisions, shoot projectiles, make items bounce off hard surfaces, and even control gravity settings so that items fall quickly or slowly. These libraries can also control the velocity of objects as they fall and often have ways to manage a body's "squishiness," or softness.

Research the various libraries available for your preferred programming language. MakeCode, for example, has some physics built in to control a sprite's velocity and acceleration. A JavaScript-based library with interesting demos is Matter.js, which can be viewed at `https://brm.io/matter-js`. Think about how you would use physics effects in games or on a web project.

Your Challenge

In this chapter, you will enhance your 3D world once again, this time by adding a physics engine so that you will be able to determine when your prowler approaches the petrified grove too closely. When the prowler gets close, the butterflies will increase their fluttering and the prowler will be pushed back.

Sketch It Out

Let's visualize the dynamic between the prowler and the butterflies by sketching it. In Figure 15.1, the sketch shows that after a collision, the prowler is repulsed!

FIGURE 15.1: A sketch of your refined A-Frame project

216

Think Like a Computer Scientist

Including a physics library will require adding some more complex interactions. This will also require you to understand how control structures work in this environment. For example, while the prowler advances toward the grove, a background process needs to be created to watch for a collision and then to react to it.

> **Definition**
>
> A *background process* is an element of a computer program that is designed to run behind the scenes without the programmer's intervention.

Rather than writing many loops to handle all kinds of positioning and reactions to collisions, you can leverage the power of imported libraries. Libraries such as the one you used to create a forest background in your A-Frame world allow you to use self-contained modules.

> **Definition**
>
> *Modules* include code that lets you pick and choose the elements you need. They can contain control structures such as loops and conditionals and are packaged in a way that lets the programmer use and reuse them throughout their programs.

In the context of A-Frame, the programmer can write their own control structures to manage the flow of the program or use imported libraries as helpers. These libraries offer their own prepackaged control structures that only need to be invoked, or called, by the programmer rather than handwritten.

Project Recipe

Start by remixing (creating a copy of) your A-Frame project from Chapter 14, "The Butterfly Brigade," in Glitch as you did in Step 1 of Chapter 14. You can rename this new project if you like. You'll be editing this new copy of your 3D world.

Step 1: Add a Physics Library

Include the ability to control the physics of your world by adding a community-built library as two scripts to the top of your `index.html` file. The first script is `ammo.js`.

> **Note**
>
> Ammo.js is a JavaScript copy, or "port," of a sophisticated physics engine called Bullet. You can read more about Bullet at `https://pybullet .org/wordpress`. Ammo.js was built using a tool to convert code to JavaScript, rather than having been done by hand. The project maintainer notes, perhaps jokingly, that AMMO stands for "Avoid Making My Own (JS physics engine by compiling Bullet from C++)."

The second script is an A-Frame physics system script that helps A-Frame use the various physics capabilities of `ammo.js` and other engines. Add the following lines in the `<head>` area of your `index.html` file, right above the closing `</head>` tag to add these scripts:

```
<script src="https://mixedreality.mozilla.org/ammo.js/
builds/ammo.wasm.js"></script>
<script src="https://cdn.jsdelivr.net/gh/n5ro/aframe-
physics-system@v4.0.1/dist/aframe-
physics-system.min.js"></script>
```

Next, you need to use these scripts in your code to make your scene be *physics aware*. To do this, edit the `<a-scene>` tag by indicating that `ammo.js` will be used. In addition, set it to be viewable in debug mode. This will draw lines around your physics objects while in debug mode so that you can more easily watch them interact. Change your `<a-scene>` opening tag to the following:

```
<a-scene physics="driver: ammo; debug: true;
debugDrawMode: 1;">
```

> **Note**
>
> Read the documentation about the ammo.js library here: `https://github.com/n5ro/aframe-physics-system`.

Step 2: Create a Periphery

Your next step is to create a periphery, which is like an invisible fence, around the grove. This will be used to prevent any prowler from actually touching the petrified wood. The easiest way to build your periphery is to create an A-Frame plane on which the grove is placed. Add the following code under the code for your camera:

```
<a-plane ammo-body="type: static" ammo-shape="type: box"
  position="2 .01 -1.5" rotation="-90 0 0" width="4"
height="2"
  color="yellow"></a-plane>
```

This plane has a few attributes. Notables are `ammo-body` and `ammo-shape`. The plane is a static body, which means that things can collide with it but it won't react to those collisions. The `ammo-shape` is the plane's footprint. The `type` of shape is `box` in this case, which is a flat, carpet-like shape that lies on the ground. If you were to change the `type` to `sphere`, the result would be a spherical shape with which you could check for airborne collisions. Since the prowler is walking on the forest floor in this world, a box `ammo-shape` works as a good enough fence. Your world should now look similar to Figure 15.2.

FIGURE 15.2: A plane added to your world

Source: Microsoft Corporation.

> **Note**
>
> The yellow color of the plane can be kept for now for debugging purposes; you can remove the color and set its opacity to 0 if you prefer not to see the plane:
>
> ```
>     <a-plane ammo-body="type: static" ammo-shape="type: box"
>         position="2 .01 -1.5" rotation="-90 0 0" width="4" height="2" opacity="0">
>         </a-plane>
> ```

Step 3: Enhance the Prowler

Now you need to make some changes to the prowling Bengal cat so that it gradually approaches the plane and then is repelled. To do this, you need to edit the cat entity code. Replace the cat `<a-entity>` with the following HTML:

```
<a-entity
        prowler
        ammo-body="type: kinematic; emitCollisionEvents:
        true;"
        ammo-shape="type: sphere; fit: manual;
        sphereRadius:.5"
        id="cat"
        scale="1.5 1.5 1.5"
        position="-2 0 -2"
        gltf-model="#cat-model"
        animation-mixer
        velocity=".1 0 0"
    >
```

You've now changed the cat to be kinematic, which means that it can be moved like a dynamic body but in a more controllable fashion.

> **Note**
>
> Read more about `ammo-body` types at `https://github.com/n5ro/aframe-physics-system/blob/master/AmmoDriver.md#ammo-body`.

We want this cat to move gradually toward the grove and then control its repulsion from the protected space. You added a sphere ammo shape (`type: sphere`) with a manual fit (`fit: manual`), so that any part of the cat's 3D body that touches the plane that was created in Step 2 will trigger a collision event.

Finally, you added a little velocity to its movement so that the Bengal cat moves gradually, in an ambling fashion, toward the plane. Your world should now look similar to Figure 15.3. Note that the cover over your animated cat that looks like a jungle gym will be removed when you turn debug mode off.

FIGURE 15.3: An approaching prowler

Source: Microsoft Corporation.

You probably noticed that the cat now moves slowly toward the plane and in fact glides right through it, disregarding the entire grove. Let's change that. You need to make some edits to better control the cat's physics interactions. To do this, you have to enhance the control structures of the actual cat component by adding JavaScript.

Turning back to DOM manipulation, as in the previous chapter, register a `prowler` component that correlates to the `prowler` HTML attribute you added to the cat entity in `index.html`. Add a file called `cat.js` to your workspace as you did in the previous chapter.

In `cat.js`, you need to register a new component called `prowler` and initialize it, attaching it to the `prowler` element in the scene. Then, you will need to add controls to do several things:

1. Grab all the elements with the butterfly class and save them to a variable called `butterflies`.

2. Add a `listener` to the entity to check if and when it collides with a static body. This listener will run in the background to test for any collision events. Then, loop through all the butterflies and set their animation speed to be faster.

3. Set the cat's attribute to go backward (velocity is now –.1) as it makes a slow retreat.

Enhance the cat component by controlling it using these steps. Add the following code to `cat.js`:

```
AFRAME.registerComponent('prowler', {
        init: function() {
            let cat = this.el;
            let sceneElement = document.querySelector('a-scene');
            let butterflies = sceneElement.querySelectorAll('.
butterfly');
            cat.addEventListener("collidestart", function () {
                //make each butterfly flap wings faster
                    for (let i = 0; i < butterflies.length; i++) {
                        butterflies[i].setAttribute('animation-
mixer','timeScale: 3.0;');
                    }
                //push the cat backwards
                cat.setAttribute('velocity', {x: -.1, y: 0, z: 0})
            });
        }
    });
```

To complete the enhancement, add `<script src="cat.js"></script>` to the `<head>` of your `index.html` before the closing `</head>` tag so that this script is initialized before the cat is added to the screen.

Step 4: Enhance the Butterfly Battalion and Complete the Scene

Now, the cat appears to bounce off the plane and slowly moves backward. But the butterflies don't yet react, because their class is not set to `butterflies`. Add one more line to `butterflies.js` above the `timeScale` attribute:

```
butterfly.setAttribute("class", "butterfly");
```

This code gives the butterflies a `class` attribute so that the cat code is able to identify the elements that have to be animated more quickly. In this context, the class of the butterfly is set to `"butterfly"`, allowing the program to identify it later as belonging to the general group of butterflies.

Congratulations! With some clever enhancements to the control structures of your world, you have made a more physics-aware, realistic vision of a special area of the forest. Now, you can turn off debugging in the `<a-scene>` tag by removing its `debug: true; debugDrawMode: 1;` attributes. You can also set the plane to have `opacity: "0"`. Watch the cat stealthily approach the grove, only to be met by the butterfly army and forced to beat a slow retreat.

Extend Your Knowledge

Explore the A-Frame physics system that is used in this tutorial and enhance your world as you like. You can find details on the physics system at `https://github.com/n5ro/aframe-physics-system`.

Add other entities to your world and make them behave in different ways. You can use characters other than the Bengal cat in your world; there are several animated GLTF (GL Transmission Format) files on the CS4Kids GitHub repo at `https://github.com/CS4Kids/sketchfab-models`. Experiment with different kinds of bodies (static, dynamic, kinematic). You can explore interesting demos of this library by going to `https://n5ro.github.io/aframe-physics-system/examples` and looking at the various examples. Explore the ammo and cannon drivers, which are both included in this library.

Vocabulary Review

In your own words, describe:

- Bodies (in a physics context)
- Collision
- Control structures
- Physics (in a web or game context)

Quiz

Select the best answer for each of the following:

Q1: A physics body that moves and reacts to collisions can be:
- a. A dynamic body
- b. A kinematic body
- c. Either of these

Q2: Code can run in the background, doing things like checking for events to happen.
- a. True
- b. False

Q3: An example of a control structure is:
- a. A loop
- b. A variable
- c. A program

Assignment: A Realistic Simulation

You've only brushed the surface of all the interesting things you can do with a good physics engine in a 3D environment. In this assignment, bring your knowledge into the real world by creating a 3D simulation of a simple action that you could do in real life. It could be a ticking metronome, a cuckoo clock, a bouncing ball, the springs on a couch, or a doughnut dropping into the fryer. Choose one element of an animated real-life object and re-create it in A-Frame as realistically as possible.

16. The Written Artifact

Standard: 2-AP-19: Document programs in order to make them easier to follow, test, and debug

You sit back and watch the creatures in your 3D world interact, bounce off barriers, advance, and retreat. The Guide also observes, curious to note the parallels between the real world and its 3D model. "It's almost as if the creatures on the screen were alive," she marvels. "Look at the cat, prowling around! It's rather magical." You agree, thinking about how you could enhance and expand this virtual world.

"But how does all the code that you wrote make all the images roam around the screen? And how does one line of code build an entire forest background? It's hard to understand," notes the Guide, puzzled. "Could you write a guide for people to understand how the pieces all fit together?" Looking back through the various pieces of code, you indeed have to think hard and remind yourself about the decisions you had to make to add lines here and there to build the world. "I think some nice documentation would be just the thing," you say. "I'll write some right away."

Do Some Research

Good documentation is a critical aspect of software development. Some programmers think that their code is so easy to read and self-explanatory that that's all you need to understand software. However, the best projects are those characterized by great documentation, also known as *docs*.

Research projects that have particularly well-written docs and make notes about why you think they are useful. Take a look, for example, at the Vue.js documentation at `https://vuejs.org/guide/introduction.html`. Figure 16.1 shows the Vue.js docs.

FIGURE 16.1: The Vue.js online documentation
Source: Evan You.

228

Notice how the layout is clean and includes a switch on the left side to pick which version of the software is featured (the API preference switch). Notice the way the topics are broken up from installation all the way to Extra Topics at the bottom. Note also the use of embedded runnable code samples illustrating simple concepts, with links to an editable playground where you can run larger sections of code and experiment with the software. Tools such as these are valuable assets that drive the adoption of Vue.js as a framework to build well-architected software.

Svelte is another open source project that has documentation online. While Svelte's technology is similar to that of Vue.js, it has a somewhat different approach for its docs. They offer documentation for folks already somewhat knowledgeable about Svelte for building websites at `https://svelte.dev/docs`, and they send those who are totally new to the technology to an interactive tutorial found at `https://svelte.dev/tutorial/basics`. What other examples can you discover and why do you consider them great docs?

Your Challenge

In this chapter you will create a set of docs as a written artifact to make understanding your 3D model easier. Your documentation will include explanations of the artifacts you used in your world, as well as instructions on how to use them. In addition, you will include graphical assets to accompany the 3D world to make it easier for others to understand what you built.

Sketch It Out

Make a list outlining the topics you believe your documentation should cover. Follow the recommendations in WriteTheDocs's Beginner's Guide, which can be found at `www.writethedocs.org/guide/writing/beginners-guide-to-docs`. Your outline might look like Figure 16.2.

① Title of project

② Running and remixing
project

③ Description of files and
libraries used

④ Contributions and support

⑤ Links to code of conduct
and license

FIGURE 16.2: A list of the documentation topics

Think Like a Computer Scientist

A terrific community called WriteTheDocs has gathered all-around best practices in documentation. The founder of this community, Eric Holscher, suggests the following ideas:

■ Documentation should be written using the same platforms used by the codebase. This concept is also called Docs As Code (`www.writethedocs` `.org/guide/docs-as-code`).

■ Documentation can be used by either users of your software or developers who want to be able to extend it. Your docs need to support both audiences.

■ Documentation should include a license, a way for people to contact you for support, a guide for contributors, a code of conduct, and a way for users to run your code.

You'll be creating new files to support these requirements and adding several elements to the `README.md` markdown file in the final A-Frame project that you created.

230

Project Recipe

In this recipe, you'll create documentation for your final 3D project. You will include comments in your code as well as add technical documentation and licensing. You will also review the inclusion of sections on contributing to the project and on support.

Step 1: Comment Your Code

While you'll be building the `README.md` file in this recipe, there's one preliminary step you can take to self-document your code: adding code comments. Code comments, which you saw in the code you wrote in the previous chapter, are notes embedded in your code that help you and others when the code is read later. These comments are an essential part of the documentation. They aren't displayed to the users of your program, but function as notes for use behind the scenes.

If you haven't already, open the 3D world Glitch project you created in the previous chapter. In `index.html` add additional HTML comments to explain potentially puzzling aspects of the code. For example, above the `prowler` entity, add:

```
<!--this is the cat prowler who collides with the plane>
```

Note that in HTML a comment starts with `<!--` and ends with `-->`. Anything between these two sets of characters is treated as a comment. Above the first `<a-scene>` tag, add:

```
<!-- turn off debug mode by removing debug and
debugDrawMode -->
```

And, above the plane, add:

```
<!-- hide this plane if preferred by removing its color
and setting opaci"y""0"-->
```

You can also add comments in the JavaScript files, using a little different pattern. In `grove.js`, for example, you can add a multiline comment at the top by adding text using the following format:

```
/* Generate many trees in this area
You can change the NUM_TREES variable in index.html
as needed.
*/
```

The `/*` indicates the start of a comment and `*/` indicates the end. You can also add a one-line comment in a JavaScript file by using two forward slashes (`//`). Any text in the same line that follows the forward slashes will be considered a comment. Add a comment similar to the following into `butterflies.js` above the attribute that sets the butterfly's class. Add this all on one line:

```
//set the class so that it can be leveraged to flap the
wings faster
```

Code comments are extremely useful when you need to revisit your own code or when others are trying to understand what you did.

Step 2: Add Technical Documentation

Now you're ready to start building the `README.md` file as a document to explain your project, so open it in Glitch. Notice that the file automatically opens in a Markdown preview view. You should click **EDIT MARKDOWN** to make any changes.

Working in the `README.md` preview file, change the title of your work from `# A-Frame Project` to something like `# Protecting the Petrified Grove`. Notice that Markdown includes several formatting helpers, with the `#` marking an `<h1>` header in the HTML that is rendered from the Markdown. Verity your work as you go by switching between the PREVIEW MARKDOWN and the EDIT MARKDOWN buttons in Glitch.

With the title changed, you now need to write your technical documentation. Feel free to deviate from the following text, which offers a basic idea of your documentation. Follow the template that you outlined in your sketch in Figure 16.2. Start with a description of the project:

```
# Protecting the Petrified Grove

---

This project was built using [A-Frame](https://aframe
.io/), a web framework for building
3D Augmented Reality or Virtual Reality experiences.

It is a 3D model of a forest scene populated by
dynamically generated cylinders of wood
simulating a small grove of petrified trees. A flock of
butterflies hover over the trees,
which lie on a plane that acts as a barrier to stop
prowlers from approaching the grove
too closely. There is animation of a Bengal cat who
gradually approaches the grove but
is repulsed when colliding with the barrier by the
flapping of the butterflies' wings.
```

Next, add a section on how a new user can run and edit the project:

```
## Running the project in a browser

You can run this project in a browser and look at its code
by Remixing it, or copying it to your own account. To do
this, click the 'Remix' button on your screen in Glitch.
```

Now, add a section on the project's features. Mention what libraries are used,
including those used for animations. Also list the files present in the project,
such as any HTML and .js files as well as its `README.md` file.

```
## Features

- index.html: This project includes several external
libraries, including A-Frame's 1.3.0
release version, Don McCurdy's A-Frame Extras library to
support building environments,
and community libraries to support physics interactions.

- butterflies.js and grove.js include JavaScript code to
dynamically generate butterflies
and the grove of trees.

- cat.js includes an extension of a 'prowler' custom com-
ponent that extends the
functionality of the bengal cat animation.

The project also includes animations from
[SketchFab](https://sketchfab.com/cs4kids/collections/
cs4kids) licensed for free usage
(see the code comments in index.html).

The project currently has debug mode enabled; to disable
it, remove `debug: true;
debugDrawMode: 1;` from the `<a-scene>` tag in index.html.
```

Step 3: Edit the License

Because you copied the original version of your project from sample code provided by A-Frame, a license file has been included, but its information is out of
date. Delete the LICENSE.md file by clicking the three-dot menu to the left of
its name. Replace the file by clicking the **+** button to open the file creation menu
and choosing the **Add License File** button as shown in Figure 16.3.

FIGURE 16.3: Generating a license

Source: Jen Looper.

> **Definition**
>
> What is a *software license*? In Chapter 13, "The Petrified Forest," you paid attention to the licenses assigned to the animated assets you chose from Sketchfab: CC-BY-4.0, a Creative Commons license. Licenses regulate how software engineers allow their software to be used. Some permissive licenses allow commercial use, and you can make money by using their software, but others forbid that kind of use. There are many different types of licenses, and it's important to understand this aspect of working in the open source area. Choose the best license for your software at `https://choosealicense.com`.

An MIT license with your name as the owner is automatically generated. An MIT license is a permissive license for software that is generally recommended for open source projects like this one.

Step 4: Add Contributing and Support Sections

Do you want other people to contribute to making your codebase better or your world more interesting? Write instructions on how you'd like people to make suggestions in this section. Some projects include a separate `CONTRIBUTING.md` guide, but since Glitch is not quite so full featured as GitHub for co-creation of content, you can simply add a few lines in a section in your `README.md` file similar to the following:

```
## Contribute

If you would like to contribute to this project, remix it
and then contact me using the
information in the section below to discuss.
```

Add a Support section as well. It's not recommended to give information about your contact details openly on the Internet, but perhaps you can point people toward a thread you want to maintain on the Glitch forum (`https://support.glitch.com`) as an area where you can discuss the project with other people:

```
## Support

If you have comments on this project, questions about it,
or suggestions on how to
improve it, please write to me on the Glitch Forum (you
can provide a link here)
```

Feel free to make this document your own and add any information you would like to present to your community.

Step 5: Add a Code of Conduct

The last file you should add will be a Code of Conduct file, which helps people who visit your software understand your preferences on their online behavior to you and to other people in the community. Glitch helpfully offers a template for this file. Generate it in the same way you generated the license file, using the button provided by Glitch to create a Code of Conduct file. This new CODE_ OF_CONDUCT.md file is created for you and populated by the Citizens Code of Conduct. Read it through to make sure you agree with and understand it. Note that the generated documentation might include your email, so you can remove that and refer users to your support section instead. The Code of Conduct file looks like Figure 16.4.

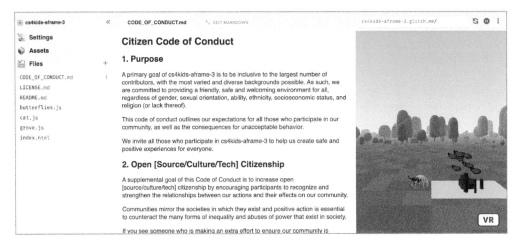

FIGURE 16.4: A Code of Conduct file
Source: Jen Looper.

238

Step 6: Link the Files

Finally, bring all your documentation together by linking to your License and Code of Conduct files from the `README.md`. At the bottom of your `README.md` file add the following:

```
## License and Code of Conduct

This software is [licensed under the MIT license](./
LICENSE.md) and includes a [Code of
Conduct](./CODE_OF_CONDUCT.md).
```

Congratulations! Your software now has all the files required to qualify it as an excellent open source project!

Extend Your Knowledge

Entire communities have grown up around open source projects, and their documentation forms an important part of their culture. Read through the documentation of a large project and look at its GitHub presence. An interesting example is the large project called Angular (`https://angular.io`) that is used to build web and mobile sites. If you visit Angular's linked GitHub repos, you find that at `https://github.com/angular/angular/issues` both the product and its documentation occupy the same repo. To keep things organized, the maintainers use tags such as `comp: docs` to triage issues pertaining to documentation.

Read through the issues tagged `comp: docs` and see how the maintainers communicate with one another, the community, and even bots to help keep documentation relevant and up to date. What do you notice about how codes of conduct are used in this context and how they ensure good behavior?

Vocabulary Review

In your own words, describe:

■ Code of Conduct

- Docs As Code
- Documentation (docs)
- License
- Open source
- `README.md` file

Quiz

The following quiz questions are to test your knowledge of the material presented in this chapter. Select the best answer for each of the following:

Q1:   It's important to include a license with your open source software because:
   a. It governs how others can use your software
   b. It allows you to make money with your software
   c. It stops others from copying your software

Q2:   Documenting your software project does which of the following?
   a. Helps explain the elements of the software
   b. Helps users use your software
   c. Both of the above

Q3:   Commenting your code is essential to help maintain it.
   a. True
   b. False

Assignment: Showcase

Build a Google Slides or Microsoft PowerPoint presentation about your project that mirrors the documentation you wrote. Use it to present the entire project from the beginning, including your flowchart, design sketches, and other decisions. Present it to an audience new to 3D modeling and see if they feel like they could build a world like yours after watching your presentation.

V
Legends of the Field Mice

17. The Field Mice

Standards:

2-AP-13: Decompose problems and subproblems into parts to facilitate the design, implementation, and review of programs

2-AP-18: Distribute tasks and maintain a project timeline when collaboratively developing computational artifacts

2-IC-22: Collaborate with many contributors through strategies such as crowdsourcing or surveys when creating a computational artifact

"I think my job is done," you say, reflecting on the work you've done to help fireflies, secure glowing moss, create a rock inventory and circulating library, and protect a fragile grove of petrified wood. "I probably should head home."

"Indeed," says the Guide, nodding in a pleased fashion. "Your work has been a tremendous help, and I'm very proud of you for taking on the challenges I've proposed." Together, you start walking along the forest path leading back to your home as the sun begins to set.

Suddenly, you hear rustling, muffled squeaks, and little scrabbling sounds in the nearby bushes. You both stop abruptly as at least 10 small mice pop out of the bushes, arranging themselves in a line to block your path. "Please, don't leave yet!" squeaks a tiny voice. Looking down, you see a portly mouse, bigger than his friends, with impressive whiskers, carrying a tiny staff made of a twig that has been whittled to size. A broad ribbon made of grass and fastened with a thistle crosses his chest. Addressing the Guide, the dignified mouse says, "Did you forget about the problems faced by the folk underground? We have an entire tunnel system that has never been properly explored and a vault that has been locked for hundreds of years. We're sure there are treasures that could be unearthed if we can just figure out how to unlock the various doors with the keys that are likely scattered throughout the passages."

"Pardon me, respected Mouse Mayor," says the Guide, apologetically. Turning to you, she says, "It's getting a little late, but are you up for this challenge?"

Of course, you are, and you follow the Mayor into the underbrush. The rest of the mice stream after you, pushing and shoving in an effort to get your attention. "There's an annoying mole in the East corner who's got something to hide," squeaks one. "Never saw the mole, but there's a scary spider in the North corridor, and it seems to be guarding something, but nobody can get past!" pipes up another. A third chimes in, "I don't know about spiders, but there's a big lake near the bottom and something is moving around in it, but we don't know what!" A baby mouse tugs at your shoelace and squeaks, "There's one place with a huge earthworm that won't let anyone pass. It's so gross!"

It sounds like this is going to be a challenging group effort to uncover the hidden secrets of this underground realm. You had better organize your work carefully so that no one is left out. By working together, you can probably get enough information to be able to unlock the vault and explore the treasure.

Do Some Research

In this chapter, you'll embark on a new kind of adventure, cataloging the underground domain of a group of field mice, each of whom has something to contribute to the story they want to tell. To do this, you'll use a free online story-building tool called Twine, available at `https://twinery.org`. But the success of your work will depend on how well you are able to gather the story elements from all the eager mice who want you to explore and unravel all the mysteries of their underground dens. This challenge resembles that experienced by data scientists or archivists who need to gather data from many different sources.

Research the ways that professionals crowdsource, or gather diverse data for, their projects. Look at some apps, such as Waze, that are good examples of crowdsourcing. Waze is a traffic app that gathers input from drivers to give warnings about accidents and potholes, for example, so that all drivers benefit. An example closer to the story challenge of this chapter is StoryCorps (`https://archive.storycorps.org`), where all kinds of people contribute to tell their own narratives. Make notes of how this data is gathered and then compiled and how crowdsourcing makes for a richer user experience.

Definition

Crowdsourcing is the task of soliciting input from many different people or groups of people using Internet resources such as forms, surveys, or other means to collect information and opinions from a large number of people.

Your Challenge

You are going to help the field mice tell their own legend, giving them a collaborative voice and helping them work together to puzzle out the mysteries of their underground tunnels. All the mice know that there is some treasure in a vault, but no one has yet been able to gather all the keys to unlock it. Some mice know about the challenges that must be surmounted to gain access to one key or another, but no one mouse knows the entire system of passages and where the keys are hidden, much less how to access them. Your job is to set up a collaborative system to gather parts of a story line and organize them into a coherent whole to unravel the mystery of this realm.

In this chapter, a partial story line is presented that could be created with the help of several assistants. You should gather a group of helpers, perhaps members of your family or classmates, to build a story line that you can input into Twine, an online story-building tool that helps you break up, or decompose, story elements. To help you in this task, you'll create a diagram of the story line using Google Drawings to organize the pieces of the story, as well as your team.

Sketch It Out

Visualize the flow of your story. Imagine that there are four passages or chambers that you need to explore, and make a diagram of how you will build this story line as a text mapping of the underground mysteries and how to solve them. Work with your collaborative team to build a diagram of four passages in an underground environment, each of which contains one of the four keys you need to unlock a vault, as well as an inventory item to help obtain the keys.

You can use Google Drawings again as you did in Chapter 13, "The Petrified Forest," this time as a collaborative tool. Log in to Google and create a new drawing by visiting `https://docs.google.com/drawings`.

> **Note**
>
> You might need to install an extension to use Google Drawings.

A new workspace is created for you with a menu of lines and shapes that you can use to build your diagram. Before starting to draw, invite the people you'd like to contribute to your story to your drawing by clicking **Share** at the top right and inviting them by email, as shown in Figure 17.1, or by sharing a link. Invite them as editors so that they will be able to add text boxes to the diagram.

Start your diagram by writing your central story idea: there is a vault that needs four keys to open. To add text to your drawing, click the Text box icon (T) in the Google Drawing menu and type the story elements into the Drawing workspace. Create your story's separate parts by adding north, south, east, and west passages as text blocks. Use the **Select line** drop-down in the same menu (▼) and choose **curved connector** to add lines between the core box and the passage boxes to indicate the flow of your story. You can add color by selecting the Line color icon in the Drawing menu (✏) and choosing the color of your preference. Your diagram might look like Figure 17.2.

246

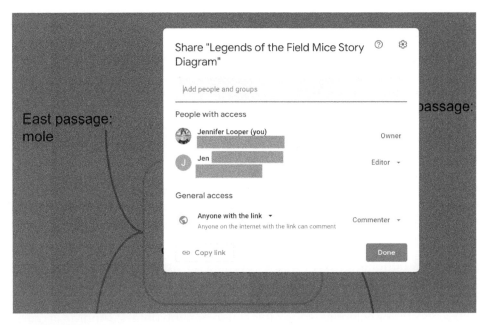

FIGURE 17.1: Inviting collaborators to your Google Drawing
Credit: Google LLC

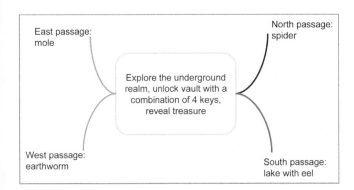

FIGURE 17.2: A diagram of the initial story elements built with Google Drawings

Think Like a Computer Scientist

In your role as crowdsourcing "content wrangler," it's your job to collect story fragments and gather them into a cohesive whole. This is a task that is accomplished in various ways by various organizations. Take a look at some of the tools used by companies to crowdsource their data.

Amazon's Mechanical Turk (`www.mturk.com`) is often used to crowdsource software tasks and data gathering. OpenIdeo (`www.openideo.com`) is a platform designed to help social impact projects come to life via crowdsourced challenges. Crowdsourcing has been put to good use by some cities, which solicit ideas to make areas of the city better, such as in London. Read more on this at `https://newcities.org/wp-content/uploads/2018/02/Crowdsourcing-the-City.pdf`.

Health care has benefited from these strategies as well. Platforms that gather data, such as 23AndMe (`www.23andme.com`), use such strategies to crowdsource ways to suggest treatment of certain genetic disorders. An interesting idea for the computer scientist is the ethical use of such data. 23AndMe is careful to include a page on data protection (`www.23andme.com/gdpr`) to explain how data will be used in compliance with privacy laws.

In the case of your story, which does not collect sensitive information, your responsibility is to credit the participants in your focus group of collaborators, which you can do when publishing your story.

Project Recipe

In this recipe, you'll build the four passages of your underground world, preparing to add conditional logic to allow keys and inventory items to be picked up and used to unlock the treasure in the ancient vault. For now, your job is to incorporate the stories suggested by your collaborators, which will likely be different from the narrative suggested here. Feel free to be creative and build your own passages and challenges to help the field mice!

Step 1: Gather All the Story Elements and Organize Your Team

Work with your collaborative team to make small outlines of each of the steps of the story that can be broken into passage elements in Twine. In this way, you can break up the work and assign parts of it to your teammates in Google.

Once you have gathered your team and everyone has access to your Google Drawing, start completing the diagram you started previously to outline the major blocks of your story. Start by asking questions of your team in the Google Drawing. Use your mouse to right-click on a word in your drawing and choose **Comment** to add prompts to help the team build the story elements. Assign the prompts to the members of your team by typing @ into the comment box. A list of the teammates you have already added will pop up so that you can select someone to respond. Your prompts will look like Figure 17.3.

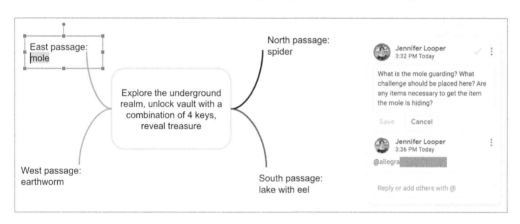

FIGURE 17.3: Adding prompts for your teammates to fill in the story elements in a Google Drawing

Credit: Google LLC.

Ask your teammates to help write all the parts of the story section, including dead ends and successful and unsuccessful decisions. Remember that there is a colored key hidden in each passage, and it's up to the explorer to acquire it. The south passage's story line, for example, might resemble Figure 17.4.

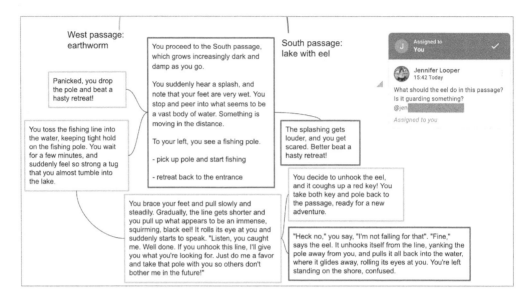

FIGURE 17.4: The parts of the South passage story line as diagrammed in Google Drawing

Credit: Google LLC.

Once you have gathered all the elements of your story for all four main passages, you can start building the interactive story in Twine.

Step 2: Set Up the Twine Environment

Now it's time to familiarize yourself with Twine. In this and the next two chapters, Twine will be used to create parts of your story. But as you and your collaborators will use your own creative ideas to unfold the narrative, we will only suggest ways to build parts of the story in Twine. This will help you get used to the way this online story-building tool works. If you get stuck, refer to the Twine reference at `http://twinery.org/reference/en`. For help learning and using Harlowe, Twine's default language, refer to the Harlowe manual at `https://twine2.neocities.org`.

In a browser, go to `https://twinery.org` and click **Use** in your browser to arrive at a welcome screen. Click through the instructions in the browser and you will find your way to the Story screen, where your stories will be saved in your browser.

> **Note**
>
> Since there is no way to log in to save your work in Twine, make sure to click the **Library > Archive** button frequently to save a copy of your work to your computer. Your work will be saved in your browser, but in case it is erased, you can always upload it back into the browser from a saved HTML file. You can archive all the stories in your Twine browser, or just one, and import one or many, as you prefer. Use the **import** link in the **Library** tab to import and restore archived versions of your stories.

Twine builds stories much as you created them in your Google Drawing, but Twine then renders them as an HTML page so that they become a clickable, "choose-your-own-adventure" story, limited only by the imagination of the writer. In the next chapter, "Lights, Sounds, Actions," you will build the logic of your inventory and key collection to open the treasure vault, but for now, concentrate on building a way for the user to enter the subterranean world and navigate to a passage.

After clicking the **Story > + New** button at the top of the browser workspace as shown in Figure 17.5, you are asked to give your new story a name.

You can call it **Legends of the Field Mice**. You are sent to a workspace for your story, as shown in Figure 17.6, with an **Untitled Passage**. Think of passages as the steps of your story or the passages or chambers of a world. Use the concept of passages to decompose the various elements of your journey through the mice's underground world.

+ New   ⌁ Edit   ⟡ Tag   ⌁ Rename   ⧉ Duplicate   🗑 Delete

0 Stories

There are no stories saved in Twine right now. To get started, you can either create a new story or import an existing one from a file.

FIGURE 17.5: The Twine story area

Credit: Twine.

Double-click the Untitled Passage box to present tools to build your passage. Click the **Rename** button and give this passage the title **Under the earth**. In the box's editing area, type the following text:

```
<h1>Legends of the Field Mice</h1>

"Come with me", squeaks a tiny voice. You look around and
discover a tiny mouse holding a
small lit torch. "But first, eat this!" says the voice.

There is a piece of cheese on a rock.

[["No, thanks!"]]
```

252

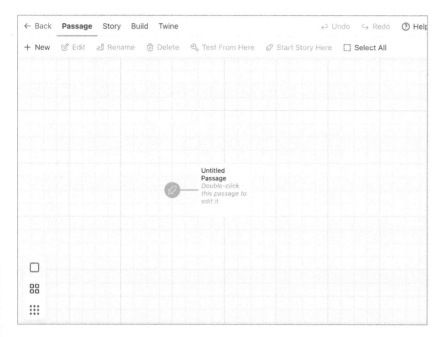

FIGURE 17.6: The first passage of your Twine story

Credit: Twine.

This text can be seen entered into Twine in Figure 17.7. Note that if you hold your mouse over parts of the code, Twine offers helpful tips.

Twine includes an editor that can help create links and other story elements rather than having you type them manually. In the passage box's menu bar shown in Figure 17.7, click **Macro** ➤ **Link** to open a dialog box, as shown in Figure 17.8. You can create links in this area linking to other areas of the story and add special effects like blurs or sliding text. Use this menu if you want to name a link other than the name of the passage, or if you want custom things to happen when links are clicked. A shortcut is to simply use double brackets to delineate links by their passage names, as in the code segment you saw earlier: `[["No, thanks!"]]`.

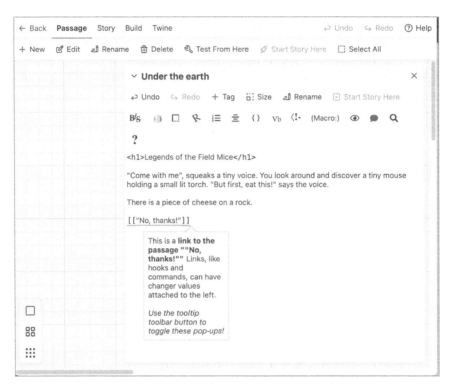

FIGURE 17.7: Building your first passage and its link

Credit: Twine.

If you click the **x** at the top right of the box, it will close and you will find that a new passage has been created for you, called "No, thanks!" as shown in Figure 17.9. This was done based on the code that you added with the double brackets called a link.

Add the text **No adventure for you today! Too bad!** in the "No, thanks!" passage's editing area. This is a dead end, but the user will be able to go back a step by using navigation that is automatically generated in a sidebar.

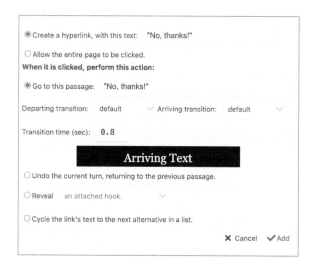

FIGURE 17.8: A menu in Twine to help build links
Credit: Twine.

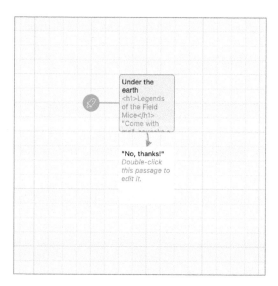

FIGURE 17.9: An autogenerated passage

Step 3: Add Hooks to Enhance Your Story's Interactivity

> **Definition**
>
> In Twine, a *hook* is a piece of text in your story that can be altered by interacting with another piece of text that is associated to a data value called a *changer*. For example, you could create a hook that makes one line of text change color when you click a different text saying "cast spell."

Go back to the "Under the earth" passage and add more code to offer the user a way forward. Underneath the link to "No, thanks!" add the text **Just take a small**. You'll complete the text by adding a hook. This hook, when clicked, will make a second piece of the passage appear.

Click the **Macros ➤ Hook** button in Twine's passage window menu to open an area where you can build the hook. The hook's name will be **action**, so add that into the Hook name area, as shown in Figure 17.10, and click the **Add** button.

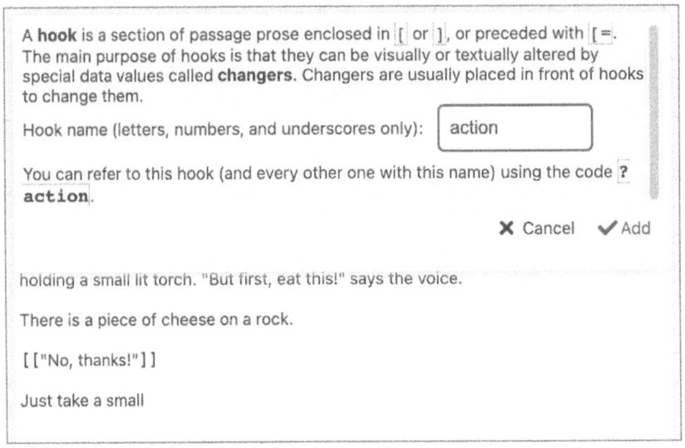

FIGURE 17.10: A hook in Twine

Credit: Twine

256

Twine generates code like the following that is appended to your passage's editing area:

```
Just take a small |action>[Your Text Here]
```

Edit the code to make the hook have a more logical link text:

```
Just take a small |action>[nibble.]
```

Step 4: Add a Changer to Your Hook

Now, you can attach an event to your hook to make something happen when you click the text **nibble**.

Definition

Events are code that will run when a hook's **action** is clicked.

Click the **Macro ➤ List All Macros** button in your passage's menu and choose **links** in the Category drop-down. Scroll down in the window and select the radio button labeled **(click: HookName or String, [Changer or Lambda])** → **Changer,** and then click the **Add** button. This selection produces the following code:

```
(click:Your Code Here)
```

Edit this code to add the hook name referenced by a ?:

```
(click: ?action)
```

Add open and close brackets ([]) after this command, as you are going to have some text and a link both display at the same time when the user interacts with the hook. Your code now looks like this:

```
(click: ?action)[]
```

> **Note**
>
> Macros in Twine are bits of code that you can call to make things happen on screen, such as setting a style, responding to a click, or opening a pop-up prompt.

Placing your mouse inside those brackets, add the `append` macro, as shown in Figure 17.11. `append` is a Macro that allows you to append text and links and other things at a specific place. Click the (**Macro > ListAll Macros** button and choose **Links**, then scroll to find **append** under the Revision heading: **(append: …HookName or String)** → **Changer**. Select this macro and click **Add**.

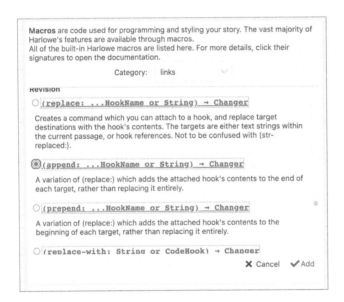

FIGURE 17.11: Adding a macro in Twine

Credit: Twine.

258

Your code now looks like this:

```
(click: ?action) [
(append:Your text here)
]
```

Edit the text to refer to the hook you created previously:

```
(click: ?action) [
(append:?action)
]
```

Add another set of brackets after the `append` macro to provide some instructions and a link to the user; these instructions show what will happen when your link is clicked. Add the text **You start to shrink! Soon, the small tunnel seems just about the right size to enter.** After this text, add a link either using the Link menu or manually so that your final code in this section looks like this:

```
Just take a small |action>[nibble.]

(click: ?action) [
(append:?action)[You start to shrink! Soon, the small
tunnel seems just about the right
size to enter.[[Go into the tunnel->Into the tunnel]]]
]
```

Let's review what the code above created:

1. You started by creating a clickable link:

   ```
   Just take a small |action>[nibble.]
   ```

   As part of creating the link, you also defined a hook called **action** that is now available in this passage to call when something needs to happen on the screen.

2. Next, you set things up so that if **action** is invoked, something should happen. In this case, the thing that happens is **append**, a macro capable of appending text and links to the screen:

```
(click: ?action)[
(append:?action)[define what should be shown on the
screen]
```

3. Finally, you defined what to append. In this case it's a text and a link to a passage. In the process, Twine created a new passage for you called **Into the tunnel**:

```
You start to shrink! Soon, the small tunnel seems just
about the right size to
enter.[[Go into the tunnel->Into the tunnel]]]
```

> **Note**
>
> These hooks and macros are a part of Harlowe, the default language to use when building Twine stories. For more information on Harlowe's special elements that help shape your story line, refer to its documentation: `https://twine2.neocities.org`.

Click **Build** ➢ **Play** at the top to open a new browser tab to play the story so far, as in Figure 17.12.

Feel free to experiment with Twine's many macros, changers, and other controls to enhance your game.

> **Note**
>
> You might need to edit the spaces between your sentences to make them more readable on the screen when rendered.

260

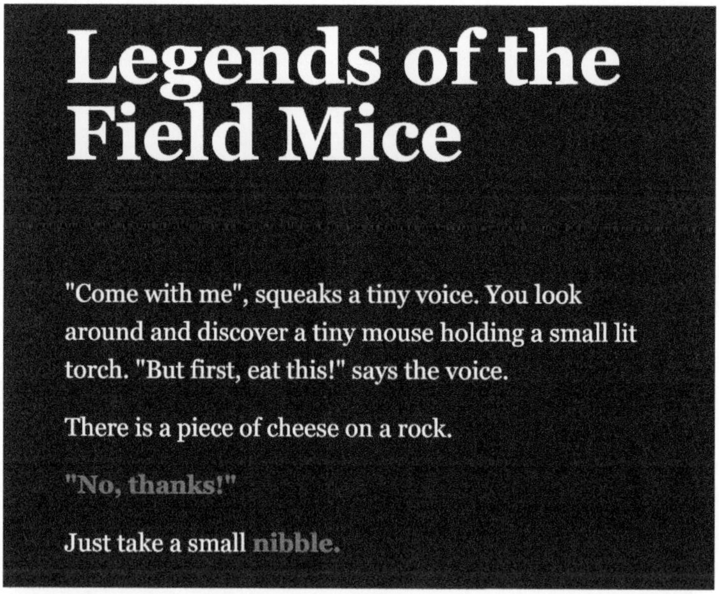

Legends of the Field Mice

"Come with me", squeaks a tiny voice. You look around and discover a tiny mouse holding a small lit torch. "But first, eat this!" says the voice.

There is a piece of cheese on a rock.

"No, thanks!"

Just take a small nibble.

FIGURE 17.12: The story so far

Step 5: Decompose the Story Line into Passages

Now, you can work parallel to your Google Drawing to translate your collaborator's story paths into Twine passages. Go to your **Into the tunnel** passage and add the following text:

```
That cheese was tasty. You wish there was more. You look
around and realize that you've
shrunk considerably and are now about three inches high.
Fortunately, your clothes shrank
as well!

Now you can follow the squeaky voice.
```

```
You are in a dark tunnel, but you seem to be able to see
pretty well.

[[Go north]]
[[Go south]]
[[Go east]]
[[Go west]]
```

Four more passages were built for you! Build the North passage with some placeholder text such as the following:

```
Proceeding north, you hear odd scrabbling sounds on the
walls. It's not reassuring.

Suddenly, your face is brushed by something sticky and you
almost tumble headfirst into a
large spider web inhabited by a big black spider!

<!--use fishing pole to whack the spider and collect key
--->

[[Suddenly remembering you have a meeting elsewhere, you
retreat back into the tunnel-
>Into the tunnel]]
```

Add the following text into the West passage:

```
You walk west, and smell something distinctly grubby,
earthy, and feel a wave of moist air. It's neither pleas-
ant nor unpleasant.

The small mouse's torch suddenly illuminates a large
earthworm that is stretched across
the passageway. You need to go around, over, or somehow
get this earthworm out of the way.
```

```
<!-- use rope to lasso the earthworm and collect key --->

[[This is all a little too much, and you retreat back into
the tunnel->Into the tunnel]]
```

Add the following text to the South passage:

```
You proceed to the south passage, which grows increasingly
dark and damp as you go.

You suddenly hear a splash and note that your feet are
very wet. You stop and peer into
what seems to be a vast body of water. Something is moving
in the distance.

<!--fishing pole logic here --->

[[This all seems fishy, and you retreat back into the
tunnel->Into the tunnel]]
```

Step 6: Add a Riddle

Build the East passage a bit more by describing the mole that inhabits this area:

```
You head toward the east passage and discover a
gentlemanly resident sitting in the
dark. He appears to have a velvet coat on and is slowly
nibbling on an insect held
delicately between his paws. Clearly almost blind, he
squints in your direction.

"You are looking for a key, I think," he says, slowly. "If
you can answer this riddle,
I'll give it to you."
```

```
"I come here in the dark of night and greet the day with
sparks of light. I bathe the earthy
stuff at dawn, but by the noon, alas! I'm gone."
```

You can add a riddle prompt so that a pop-up box will open in Twine to accept riddle guesses. Start by adding a `temp` variable into the East passage. This temporary variable will only exist in this passage, as opposed to global variables, which can be referenced from all passages. Create a variable by clicking **Macros ➤ Value** in the East passage's menu to open a box. Call this variable **answer**, as shown in Figure 17.13.

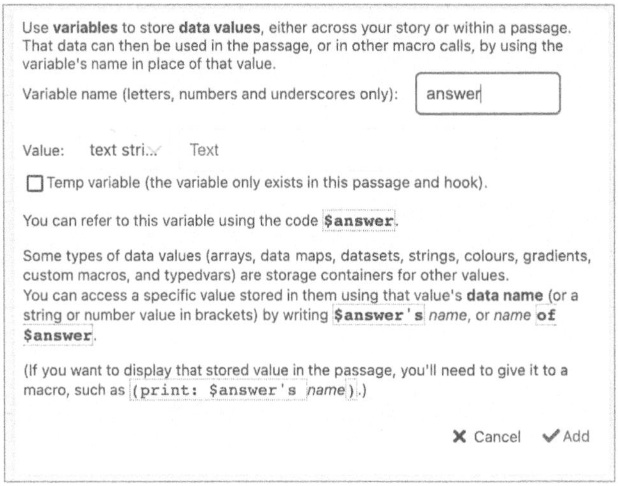

FIGURE 17.13: Adding a temp variable in Twine
Credit: Twine.

Leaving the value box empty, add this variable and click the **Add** button to close the window. Then, add the following text at the bottom of the main input area of this passage to give context to the riddle input box you want to build:

```
Add your answer in the box and click the link underneath.
```

Right after that text, add an input box by clicking the **Macro ➤ Input** button in the Twine menu. An area to build your input box opens, as shown in Figure 17.14.

264

Bind the value of this input box to the `temp` variable you just set by selecting the **Bind** check box, choosing _ in the variable type drop-down (since it references the `temp` variable **answer**), and add **answer** as the variable to match to any entries in this text box.

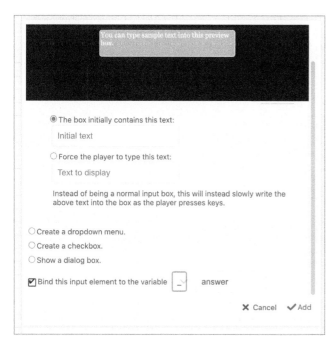

FIGURE 17.14: Adding an input box in Twine
Credit: Twine.

Here is the code so far for this section:

```
(set: _answer to "")
```

```
Add your answer in the box and click the link underneath
(input-box:2bind _answer,"=XX=")
```

Next, add logic to handle both correct and incorrect text box inputs. Create a link macro with open brackets surrounding open curly braces so that you can create a conditional:

```
(link:"Answer the riddle")[{}]
```

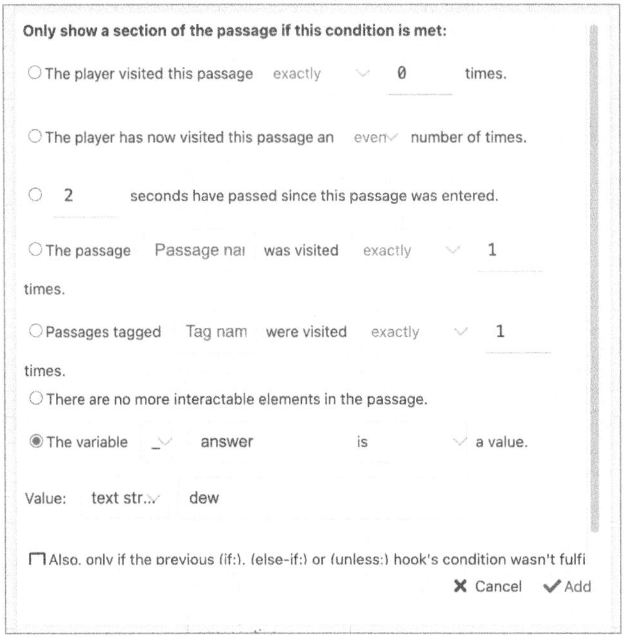

FIGURE 17.15: Adding a conditional in Twine

Credit: Twine

Then, place your mouse inside the curly braces and click the **Macro ➤ If** button in the passage's menu. Select the variable radio button and set it to ensure that the _answer is **dew**. Click the **Add** button as in Figure 17.15.

The code that is generated is incomplete:

```
(if:_answer is "dew")[Your Text Here]
```

266

Macros are code used for programming and styling your story. The vast majority of Harlowe's features are available through macros.
All of the built-in Harlowe macros are listed here. For more details, click their signatures to open the documentation.

Category: navigation   ⌄

Navigation

◉ (go-to: String) → Command

This command stops passage code and sends the player to a new passage, starting a new turn as if a passage link was clicked. If the passage named by the string does not exist, this produces an error.

○ (redirect: String) → Command

This command sends the player to a new passage. However, unlike (goto:), this does *not* start a new turn - undoing after this will send the player to the turn before the redirect occurred.

○ (undo: [String]) → Command

This command stops passage code and "undoes" the current turn, sending the player to the previous visited passage and forgetting any variable changes that occurred in this passage. You may provide an optional string to display if undos aren't available.

✕ Cancel   ✔ Add

FIGURE 17.16: Adding a navigation to a new passage in Twine
Credit: Twine

Overwrite the `Your Text Here` placeholder by deleting it and adding a go-to macro. Place your mouse between the if conditional's brackets and click **Macro ➢ List All Macros** in Twine's menu. Choose the **navigation** category in the top drop-down of the editor and select **go-to**, as shown in Figure 17.16. Click **Add**.

Your generated code now looks like the following:

```
(link:"Answer the riddle")[{(if:_answer is "dew")[(go-to:Your Code Here)]}]
```

Complete this logic by adding an else conditional. Just before the close of the final curly braces, add this line:

```
(else:) [
        (go-to: Your Code Here)
    ]
```

Your conditional now looks like the following code:

```
(link:"Answer the riddle")[{
(if:_answer is "dew")[
    (go-to:Your Code Here)]
(else:) [
    (go-to: Your Code Here)]
}]
```

Step 7: Complete the East Passage

Let's review! In the East passage, you added a pop-up prompt to oblige the user to answer the riddle correctly, after which the user is directed to either the correct or the incorrect passage, where they will be able to collect a key if their answer is correct. Because the user gains access to these passages only if they can answer a riddle, and not by a link, you will need to add the Correct! and Incorrect! passages manually. Click the **Passage ➢ New** button in the top menu and add one passage called **Correct!** and another called **Incorrect!**.

Add the following text to the Correct! passage's code:

The mole smiles and hands you a green key attached to a long coil of rope.

Add the following text to the Incorrect! passage's code:

The mole shakes its head slowly.

Then, edit the conditional in your East passage riddle to refer to these passages:

```
(link:"Answer the riddle")[{
(if:_answer is "dew")[
    (go-to: "Correct!")]
(else:) [
    (go-to: "Incorrect!")
]
}]
```

268

The last thing you need to do is add a link at the bottom of the East passage to allow the user to retreat:

```
[[You hate riddles, and you retreat back into the tunnel-
>Into the tunnel]]
```

The entire code for the East passage looks like the following:

```
You head toward the east passage, and discover a
gentlemanly resident sitting in
the dark. He appears to have a velvet coat on and is
slowly nibbling on an insect held
delicately between his paws. Clearly almost blind, he
squints in your direction.

"You are looking for a key, I think," he says, slowly. "If
you can answer this riddle, I'll give it to you."

"I come here in the dark of night and greet the day with
sparks of light. I bathe the earthy stuff at dawn, but by
the noon, alas! I'm gone."

(set: _answer to "")

Add your answer in the box and click the link underneath
(input-box:2bind _answer,"=XX=",1)

(link:"Answer the riddle")[{
    (if:_answer is "dew")[
        (go-to: "Correct!")
    ]
    (else:) [
        (go-to: "Incorrect!")
    ]
}]
```

```
[[You hate riddles, and you retreat back into the tunnel-
>Into the tunnel]]
```

In the next chapter, you'll learn more about how to build an inventory and collect items to solve the puzzle of the locked vault. For now, you have scaffolded the building blocks of your adventure following your collaborators' suggestions. Your Twine story should now look similar to Figure 17.17.

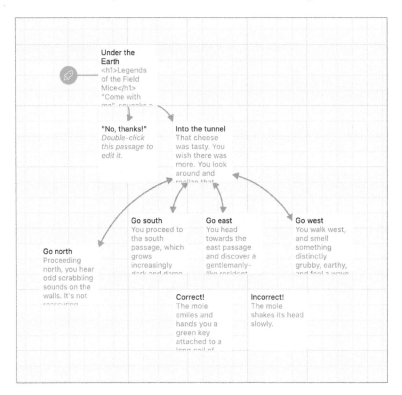

FIGURE 17.17: The game in Twine so far

Congratulations! You have the beginnings of an amazing four-part choose-your-own-adventure text story built in Twine. Make sure to put your own personal stamp on it and tell the narrative you, and your collaborators, have designed.

Vocabulary Review

In your own words, describe:

- Crowdsource
- Decomposition

Quiz

The following quiz questions are to test your knowledge of the material presented in this chapter. Select the best answer for each of the following:

Q1: Decomposing elements of your work allows you to:
   a. Break up tasks into smaller parts that can be more easily done
   b. More easily collaborate with teammates who can be assigned, or choose, to do smaller parts of a project
   c. Both of these

Q2: What is crowdsourcing?
   a. Assigning licenses to crowds
   b. Requesting assistance and collaboration from communities
   c. Asking a crowd of people questions

Q3: Airbnb could be considered an example of crowdsourcing.
   a. True
   b. False

Assignment: Storytime

Continue to flesh out your collaboration and the story that you are building as a group. Build your various passages, pauses, chambers, and other elements of your story as blocks in Twine. By the end, you should have four passages, some with dead-end choices and some leading to challenges that must be met to acquire inventory items and keys.

18. Lights, Sounds, Action

Standards:

2-AP-14: Create procedures with parameters to organize code and make it easier to reuse

2-AP-18: Distribute tasks and maintain a project timeline when collaboratively developing computational artifacts

The little mice encircle you as you explore the underground labyrinth. Maybe you should have brought some thread to mark your way so you wouldn't get lost. At any rate, the little helpers, talking excitedly, pull on your arm to guide you to the various passages where there are puzzles to solve. As you explore, you start to realize that the tunnel is not a flat, black space. There are contours, passages with some light, stones, blocked outlets, dead ends, and more. It is a much more varied landscape than you had previously thought. You start to notice sounds and smells, including a dripping sound in the distance and odd scratching noises.

You start to collect items that you think might be helpful in getting past the various challenges you meet, including a fishing pole that doubles as a club and a rope that can be used as a lasso.

"And don't forget the vault," notes the Mouse Mayor as he walks by your side. "It's never been opened, but there are four keyholes. If you can collect the keys to this vault, we'll be able to open it and see what's inside." Sure of your mission, you continue to explore.

Do Some Research

In this chapter, you'll continue to build out the parts of your story line, including adding some custom JavaScript that you can call from your passages.

273

As your codebase expands, so can the complexity of your code, a problem often called *spaghetti code* by programmers. Have you ever written code, designed a system, or created pseudocode that felt like spaghetti because it tends to have no logical flow and a lot of isolated functions? Did you write programs in earlier chapters that could be made easier to read and understand now with some rewriting? How would you rewrite it to make it cleaner, more readable, and easier to maintain? Read about other "pasta antipatterns" in the article referenced below and see if your code bears a resemblance.

> **Note**
>
> According to the article "Fix Spaghetti Code and Other Pasta-Theory Antipatterns" at TechTarget (`www.techtarget.com/searchsoft-warequality/tip/Fix-spaghetti-code-and-other-pasta-theory-antipatterns`), there is a whole "pasta theory" of code, including spaghetti, lasagna, pizza, and ravioli code.

Your Challenge

Build on the world that you started to create in Twine, with the North, South, East, and West passages delineated. This time, you'll add in the ability to collect and display inventory items and keys so as to get access to the vault. You'll also add sounds and enhance the visual interest of the game using a clean code pattern by adding a graphic as a background to change depending on the passage.

Sketch It Out

Add to your Google Drawing diagram by asking your contributors to look for free images that can be used as backdrops for each passage group. Since you will be developing code that can display the images, you need to work asynchronously with your collaborators.

Use a new Google Drawing or add to your current one. Draw a long horizontal arrow using the Line item in the menu. Add text boxes showing the days and/ or times by which you need your backdrops chosen. Right-click each text box and add a comment for each work item, assigning it to a person on your collaboration team. Ask them to provide links to free images that would look good as backdrops. You can ask them to drop the image itself into your document by using Insert image from the Drawing menu. Your diagram might look like Figure 18.1.

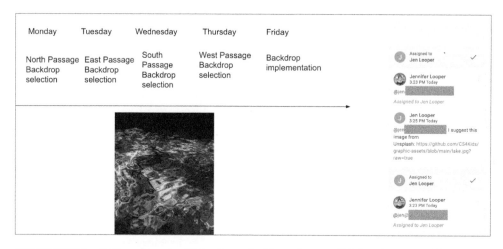

FIGURE 18.1: A timeline built in Google Drawings with background images delineated

Credit: Google LLC

Think Like a Computer Scientist

In previous chapters, the importance of refactoring and following don't repeat yourself (DRY) patterns was discussed, as well as decomposing your code design to create small building blocks. Twine allows you to customize the look of your story using Cascading Style Sheets (CSS). Twine allows you to use custom JavaScript, which you can use to enhance your project. You'll find boxes where you can enter custom JavaScript and CSS code in the Story area of your Twine workspace. While it's tempting to start pasting (or using *copypasta,* as some developers call it) interesting snippets into the JavaScript box in Twine, be careful to maintain readable code. The same rules for writing quality code apply in Twine, which has its own limitations and syntax to follow.

It's useful to think about how you could simplify code by rewriting it. The website `https://refactoring.guru/refactoring` offers interesting challenges and examples of all kinds of code rewriting tasks. Pick a few examples and see if any of your code contains what is termed a *code smell*—a characteristic that will cause problems down the road.

Project Recipe

In this recipe, you'll enhance your Twine story to include the ability to collect inventory items so as to acquire keys that will allow you to unlock the vault. You'll also use a reusable function to create more interesting backdrops for your passages. Finally, you'll have the option to include sounds by adding the HAL-Audio library to your Twine app.

Step 1: Add the Startup and Inventory Passages

Many games have a way for a player to gather items, like keys or coins, that can be used as the game progresses. In Twine, you can build an inventory library as a separate passage where items are stored. To add inventory-gathering capabilities to your Twine app, you need to create two new unlinked passages, which will function as a footer and a startup script. Click the **Passage** ➤ **New** button at the top-left corner of the Twine workspace and add the two

276

passages. Rename them by clicking their **rename** buttons. The first will be called **Startup**. Add the following code to this new passage:

```
(set: $inventory to (a:))
(set: $keys to (a:))
```

> **Note**
>
> You can use the Twine buttons to create variables and the pop-up helper menu to create these snippets if you prefer.

This code creates two new empty arrays called **$inventory** and **$keys**, where you will be able to store any inventory and keys that you pick up in the passages. Create a tag called **startup** by clicking **+Tag** at the top left of the passage editing dialog box. Name the tag **startup**, and then click **Add** to save it. This tag designates this passage as something that runs before the app starts, as shown in Figure 18.2.

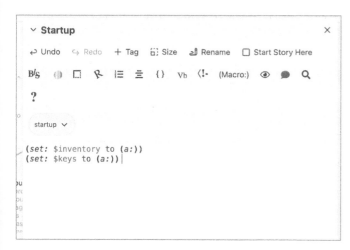

FIGURE 18.2: Creating a tagged startup passage
Credit: Twine

Create another unlinked passage in the same way, this one called **Inventory** with a tag called **footer**, so that Twine is told where it should be placed on the screen. Add the following code, as shown in Figure 18.3:

```
<hr/>

Your inventory contains (if: $inventory's length > 0)

[(print: (joined: ", ", ...$inventory))]

(else:)[ nothing yet ]

and you have collected (if: $keys's length > 0)[ (print:
(joined: ", ", ...$keys))]

(else:)[ no keys yet ]
```

In this code, you are listing any inventory items that you collect as you go through the game. As you pick up items and keys, they are added to the inventory and keys arrays. If there is nothing in those arrays, the footer notes that you have not collected them yet.

If you prefer all the inventory items to show on one line rather than being divided up onto different lines, you can compress the code as shown in Figure 18.3. If it's easier for you, create this snippet using Twine's **if** and **macro** buttons to create the conditionals and print some text to the screen.

FIGURE 18.3: Creating a tagged footer passage displaying inventory items

Credit: Twine

Step 2: Add Inventory

> **Note**
>
> In the assignment in Chapter 17, "The Field Mice," you were tasked with building your passages with the help of your team. In this section, you'll build a story line that shows how to pick up and drop inventory items, but feel free to use your own story elements as they evolve.

Now, you can start adding moments into your Twine story where your user can pick up or drop items. Let's enhance the **Go south** passage so that the user can pick up or discard a fishing pole and get a key.

Open the **Go south** passage and note the comment where you can add fishing pole logic. Add the following text at that point by either typing it by hand or using Twine's menu buttons. It should look like the following:

```
(if: ($inventory contains 'a fishing pole')) [
It seems as if you've already been here. Better [[go back->
Under the earth]]
] (else:) [
Do you want to pick it up?
{ (link: 'Pick up the pole.') [
        (set: $inventory to $inventory + (a: "a fishing
pole"))
(goto: 'Fishing')
] }]
```

In this snippet, you added a conditional to check whether you already have the fishing pole:

```
if: ($inventory contains 'a fishing pole')) [
```

If you don't have a fishing pole in your inventory, you are asked to pick it up with the text `Do you want to pick it up?`

If the user clicks this text, the pole is added to your inventory, and you can navigate to the next block.

Since you used `goto: 'Fishing'` to navigate to the passage "Fishing," you'll need to create that passage manually, so add a new passage called **Fishing** by clicking the **Passage ➤ New** button at the top left of the workspace.

Add the following code to the Fishing passage:

```
You toss the fishing line into the water, keeping tight
hold on the fishing pole. You
wait for a few minutes, and suddenly feel so strong a tug
that you almost tumble into the
```

lake.

```
[[Drop the pole->Drop the pole]]
[[Pull!->Catch the eel]]
```

Note that two new passages were created when you added this code. In the **Drop the pole** passage, add the ability to remove the pole from your inventory by adding the following code:

```
Panicked, you drop the pole and beat a hasty retreat!

(set: $inventory to $inventory - (a: "a fishing pole"))
[[Go back->Go south]]
```

Here, you removed the fishing pole from the inventory array using the following code:

```
(set: $inventory to $inventory - (a: "a fishing pole"))
```

You also added a link to go back to the **Go south** passage. In the **Catch the eel** passage, add the following code:

```
You brace your feet and pull slowly and steadily. Gradu-
ally, the line gets shorter, and
you pull up what appears to be an immense, squirming,
black eel! It rolls its eye at you
and suddenly starts to speak. "Listen, you caught me. Well
done. If you unhook this line,
I'll give you what you're looking for. Just do me a favor
and take that pole with you so
others don't bother me in the future!"


[[Refuse->Refuse]]
[[Unhook the eel->Unhook the eel]]
```

Two more passages have been added: **Refuse** and **Unhook the eel**! In **Refuse**, add the following code to lose the fishing pole again:

```
"Heck no," you say, "I'm not falling for that". "Fine,"
says the eel. It unhooks itself from the line, yanking the
```

```
pole away from you and pulls it all back into the water,
where it glides away, rolling its eyes at you. You're left
standing on the shore, confused.
(set: $inventory to $inventory - (a: "a fishing pole"))
[[go back->Into the tunnel]]
```

And finally, in the **Unhook the eel** passage, discover your reward with the following code. This code will add a red key to the keys list:

```
You decide to unhook the eel, and it coughs up a red key!
You take both key and pole back to the passage, ready for
a new adventure.
(set: $keys to $keys + (a:'a red key'))
[[go back->Into the tunnel]]
```

Your story in the Twine workspace now looks something like Figure 18.4, although the boxes might be in different places. When you click **Play** to walk through your story, you can retrieve a fishing pole and a red key, which are displayed in the footer, as shown in Figure 18.5.

You can also enhance the **Go east** passage that you started so that when the mole's riddle is guessed correctly and you are taken to the **Correct!** passage, a coil of rope and a green key are collected. Edit the **Correct!** passage in this area:

```
(set: $keys to $keys + (a:'a green key'))
(set: $inventory to $inventory + (a:'a coil of rope'))
[[Go back->Go east]]
```

In the next chapter you will create some logic such that certain inventory items are necessary to collect keys.

Step 3: Add a Background Image

While building your winding Twine story is a great exercise in itself for breaking down elements and adding code passage by passage, you want to make your code clean and readable as you go as well. Since you want to create an interesting world both textually and visually, it's useful to be able to change the backdrops to visually improve your passages. To help you with switching backdrops in your passages, you can make a neat function that will accept an image parameter so that you won't have to add images manually to each passage.

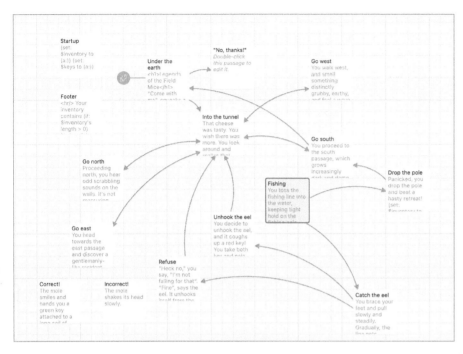

FIGURE 18.4: Your Twine application so far
Credit: Twine

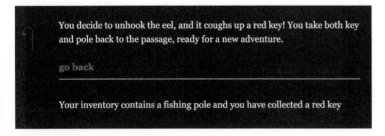

FIGURE 18.5: Collecting inventory items
Credit: Twine.

Start by opening the central area where the application styles can be edited globally. At the top of the Twine workspace, choose **Story** ➢ **Stylesheet** to add styles that will darken the background behind your story text so that it will be more readable when you add an image background and position the background itself. Add the following code to the displayed stylesheet:

```
tw-passage {
  background-color: black;
    padding: 10px;
    border-radius: 5px;
    opacity: 70%;
}

tw-story {
  background-position: center;
    background-repeat: no-repeat;
    background-size: cover;
}
```

This code allows each page of the story to accept a background image that won't be repeated but will cover the entire page. In addition, since you want the white text of your story to show up well even if there's a background image, you set the background behind the text blocks to be black, mostly opaque so that the background shows through a little, with a rounded border. You can edit this code if you prefer different colors or styles.

Now, click **Story** ➢ **JavaScript** in the same menu. In this area, you add all the reusable JavaScript code that is available throughout the story. Add one function that takes an image path as a parameter:

```
function changeBackground(image) {
  document.querySelector("tw-story").style.backgroundImage
= `url("${image}")`;
}
window.changeBackground = changeBackground;
```

This code can now be called from any passage, and you can pass in a new image background to be set in that particular area. You can place a new image,

284

for example, for each North, South, East, and West passage and the background will be retained throughout the child passages. For example, to change the background image in the **Under the earth** passage, add the following call to the `changeBackground()` function, setting a mouse image as the background:

```
<script>changeBackground("https://github.com/
CS4Kids/graphic-
assets/blob/main/mouse.jpg?raw=true")</script>
```

Similarly, reuse the function in the **Into the tunnel** passage, setting a tunnel image as the passage's background:

```
<script>changeBackground("https://github.com/
CS4Kids/graphic-
assets/blob/main/tunnel.jpg?raw=true")</script>
```

Finally, in the **Go south** passage use the function again by adding the following call to `changeBackground` and the image `lake.jpg`:

```
<script>changeBackground("https://github.com/
CS4Kids/graphic-
assets/blob/main/lake.jpg?raw=true")</script>
```

> **Note**
>
> These images are linked to images found on `https://unsplash.com` and saved with attribution to the CS4Kids GitHub repo. If you decide to use your own images, save them to a place where you can give them proper attribution and use them in your code by replacing the image path with your own.

Your story now has some interesting backdrops, such as the one shown in Figure 18.6, built with reusable, clean code that is stored centrally and called from passages when needed. Well done!

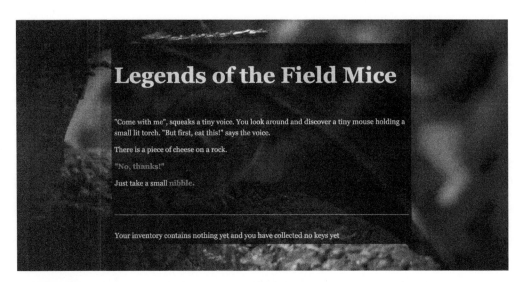

FIGURE 18.6: Your Twine story with a backdrop
Credit: Google LLC

Extend Your Knowledge

In this optional section, you can add audio to your Twine app by including an external community build library called HAL-Audio, specially designed for Harlowe Twine apps. The documentation for this library is found at `https://twinelab.net/harlowe-audio/#`. This exercise will allow you to get to know how to use external libraries in the online Twine environment, in case you want to extend your app in this way.

1. Download the HAL-Audio library from GitHub at `https://github.com/ChapelR/harlowe-audio/releases` and unzip the files. You'll find a JS and a CSS file in this zip.

2. Create a new stand-alone passage in your story using **Passage** ➤ **New**. Rename it **hal.tracks** and add the following code to the **hal.tracks** passage:

```
water: https://github.com/CS4Kids/graphic-assets/blob/
main/water.mp3?raw=true
```

286

3. Open the JavaScript window in Twine's workspace by clicking the name of your application in the bottom-left corner and choosing **Story ➤ JavaScript**. Open the `harlowe-audio.min.js` file using a text editor like TextEdit or Notepad from the zip archive you downloaded and paste the contents of the file into the bottom of the JavaScript window.

4. Likewise, open the CSS window in the workspace and choose **Story ➤ Stylesheet**. Open `harlowe-audio.min.css` from the zip archive you downloaded and paste its contents into the bottom of the CSS window.

5. Finally, paste the following code into the **Go south** passage, where you want your audio to start:

```
{
(track: 'water', 'loop', true)
(track: 'water', 'playwhenpossible')
}
```

If you click **Play** to view your story, you'll notice a pop-out menu, as shown in Figure 18.7, that you can use to control your audio manually, added when you edited the CSS.

You'll also find that a water sound starts playing when you enter the South passage. To further control audio and change sounds that play, enhance your app by adding conditionals around your sounds, as outlined at `https://twinelab.net/harlowe-audio/#/?id=checking-if-a-sound-is-already-playing`.

FIGURE 18.7: The audio menu
Credit: Google LLC

> **Note**
>
> Pay attention to the licensing restrictions in the images and sounds that you use in your work, as some might not be usable for your purpose.

Congratulations! You have built and enhanced a storytelling application with Twine. In the next chapter, you will work with your team to complete the project and unlock the mysterious vault!

Vocabulary Review

In your own words, describe:

- Code smells
- Spaghetti code

Quiz

The following quiz questions are to test your knowledge of the material presented in this chapter. Select the best answer for each of the following:

Q1:   Writing your code as reusable elements allows you to:
   a. Make your code more readable
   b. Make your code more maintainable
   c. Both of these

Q2:   A parameter can be used in a function to:
   a. Reuse the function
   b. Create switches in the code
   c. Pass in a value for processing

Q3:   A so-called "code smell" is a characteristic in the code that:
   a. Features decomposition
   b. Causes degradation of the code
   c. Will cause problems down the road as it is badly written

Assignment: Building Inventory

Continue to complete your own version of your story about the underground world as you progress through the passages, adding various moments where you can collect and drop inventory items. You can even add dead ends where a dropped item causes some problem and the passage has to be restarted. Be as creative as you like, remembering that in the next chapter we will be adding a way for the collection of some keys to be contingent on the collection of certain items, so plan your story accordingly.

19. Unlocking the Vault

Standard: 2-AP-16: Seek and incorporate feedback from team members and users to refine a solution that meets user needs

You've worked hard to solve riddles, gather equipment, and win the four colored keys that will help you open the mysterious underground vault that has been closed for years. The excitement of the crowds of mice encircling you is palpable. They squeak eagerly, tugging at your hand and leading you to a vast opening in the tunnel network. There, you spy a rusty, peeling hunk of metal. "That's the vault?" you say, somewhat crestfallen. Somehow you expected something more impressive.

"Indeed it is!" says the Mayor, "and never in my time in office have I ever had a chance to see what's inside. Please, don't delay, use the keys to open the vault!"

The mice swish their tails and whiskers in anticipation. "Hold on a minute," you say, grasping the keys tightly in your hand. "What if there's something really valuable in the vault? Who will get it? Who will it belong to?"

The Mayor clears his throat. "Well, obviously it belongs to me," he says. There is an immediate uproar of indignant mice commentary.

"That's not fair! It should benefit everyone! It should be invested! It should only benefit the residents of the nearby tunnels!" Shouts fill the air. You hadn't meant to incite a riot, and you're sorry you mentioned it. "Let's do this fairly!" you say loudly, over the hubbub, "and put it to a vote."

Do Some Research

User-centered design considers the requirements and needs of a diverse variety of users. In the case of the mice, the entire community wants a say in how the vault should be accessed. Similarly, communities often ask for the ability to help shape products. Research how creators ask for advice to make their products better and how they incentivize their users to give feedback. A good place to start is ProductHunt, which you can visit at `http://producthunt.com`.

Definition

User-centered design is a methodology that enables designers to build software gradually, based on feedback gathered progressively from the software's current or future users. According to the Interaction Design Foundation, "User-centered design is an iterative process that focuses on an understanding of the users and their context in all stages of design and development." Read more at `www.interaction-design.org/literature/topics/user-centered-design`.

For a good example of how a product team used the ProductHunt platform to get feedback about the second version of their software, take a look at the launch of the popular note-taking tool called Notion, which had a ProductHunt launch recorded at `www.producthunt.com/products/notion#notion-2-0`. Notice how the ProductHunt interface allows for direct interaction between creators and users, and how users can upvote, or recommend, other users' helpful reviews.

Research other ways that companies seek and incorporate user feedback, taking note of the many ways that they use polls, surveys, email newsletters, and other ways of outreach. How does Amazon make use of user feedback? How about Spotify? TikTok? When is it obvious that they are gathering and using feedback to make their products better, and when is it less obvious? Do you prefer to be aware when your interactions on a website or mobile app provide feedback to a company?

Your Challenge

In this final chapter about the underground realm, you'll develop a way to poll your users to create the best ending for your story, which you will then build to complete your Twine story. This will once and for all determine what, if anything, is in the mysterious vault. In the process, you'll build two forms to crowdsource possible endings to your story and then complete the ending, making sure that you have successfully gathered all four keys before attempting to open the vault.

Sketch It Out

Make a quick list of possible story endings that you believe would be interesting to build. Your list might look like Figure 19.1.

Think Like a Computer Scientist

Gathering user feedback and using it to make product decisions forms a large part of work around user experience (UX). Decisions need to be made at the design stage regarding how feedback will be gathered. Will it be gathered implicitly by building feedback mechanisms into the software itself, or will it be gathered explicitly by asking your users to provide it? An implicit feedback process might involve behind-the-scenes work that could impact the performance of your software.

You want your products to meet the needs of your users, so you might be asked to gather statistics from within your product itself about how it is being used. You could implement a solution like Google Analytics that functions in the background, tracking clicks and scrolls to check where users pause and where they scroll past items on the screen. Alternately, you could add a feedback button, a rating mechanism, or a live chat area for users to interact more directly with your website for instant built-in feedback.

A more explicit way of gathering feedback is to interact with people on social media, whether on Twitter, TikTok, Instagram, Facebook, or another site.

On these sites, you can directly interact with your website's user base, asking questions and gathering their opinions.

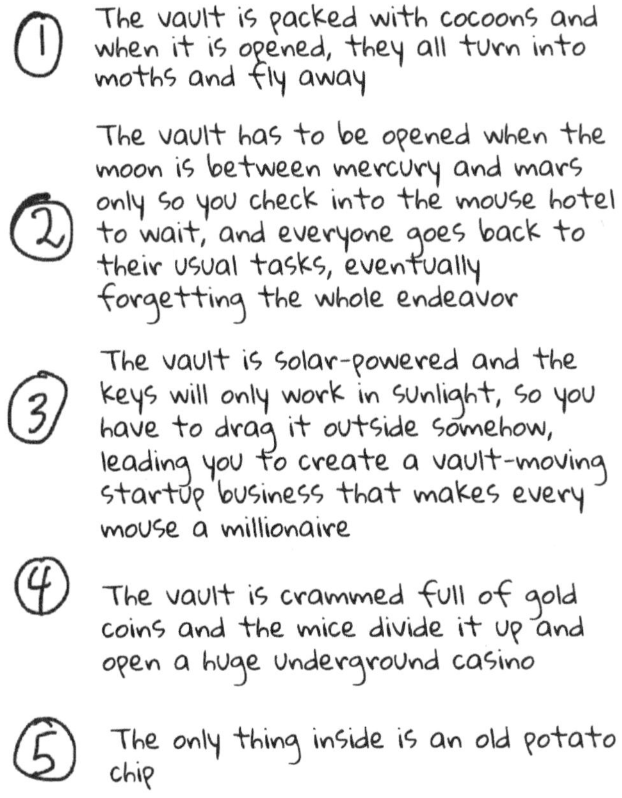

(1) The vault is packed with cocoons and when it is opened, they all turn into moths and fly away

(2) The vault has to be opened when the moon is between mercury and mars only so you check into the mouse hotel to wait, and everyone goes back to their usual tasks, eventually forgetting the whole endeavor

(3) The vault is solar-powered and the keys will only work in sunlight, so you have to drag it outside somehow, leading you to create a vault-moving startup business that makes every mouse a millionaire

(4) The vault is crammed full of gold coins and the mice divide it up and open a huge underground casino

(5) The only thing inside is an old potato chip

FIGURE 19.1: A list of potential endings for the story

There are trade-offs to both strategies. Implicit feedback may cause your website to slow down or clutter the screen, as software needs to be installed and running to get these widgets, analytics, polls, and chats to work. You don't want to annoy your users to the point that they regret trying your product! Explicit feedback, on the other hand, may be biased, spotty, or anecdotal. Either way, establishing a good rapport with the folks who use the software you develop is essential and will help improve it in the long run.

Project Recipe

In this recipe, it is assumed that you have built the North, South, East, and West passages of your story in Twine as shown in the previous chapter, and that your story is lacking only the final ending where the keys are used to open the vault. You'll write the ending by gathering user feedback and then choosing the best solution, voted on by your community, to build the end of the story.

Step 1: Publish Your Story

Continuing your work from Chapter 18, "Lights, Sounds, Action," open your Twine workspace in a browser. Your job now is to get user feedback, so you need to publish your story somewhere for people to access it easily. In the bottom-left corner, click the **Build** ➤ **Publish to File** option in the top menu bar. An HTML file is generated and downloaded to your computer.

Go to Glitch.com, with which you should be familiar after working with it in Chapters 17, "The Field Mice," and 18, "Lights, Sound, Action." Sign into your account on Glitch and click the top-right **New Project** button. A drop-down menu opens; choose the **glitch-hello-website** template. Your new project will be built and will include several files.

Locate the file that you saved from Twine. Drag it into the Glitch workspace in your new project or click **Files** in the left menu and choose **upload a file**. Delete the existing `index.html` file by holding your mouse over the filename and using the three-dot menu on the right to choose **delete**. Then, rename the Twine file that you uploaded, using the same three-dot menu, but this time choose **rename**. Rename your file **index.html**.

Once you rename your new `index.html` file, you'll be able to access the new address of your website as a `glitch.me` file. View this new site by navigating to the preview pane of your Glitch site and, at the top right of the window, use the three-dot menu to choose **Open in new window**, as shown in Figure 19.2. The website that opens has a URL that you can now share anywhere so that anyone can enjoy your story. Be sure to make a note of the web address to share in the form you'll build next.

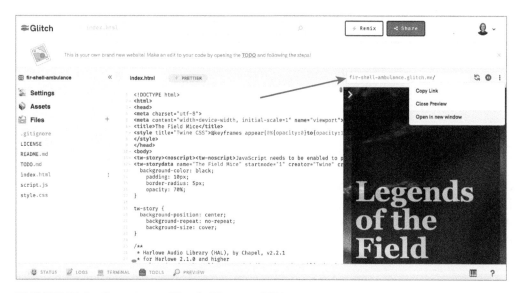

FIGURE 19.2: Opening a Glitch file as a URL
Credit: Glitch

Step 2: Gather Story Ending Suggestions

Now you can prepare to gather feedback from your team about the best way to finish your story. Start by building your first form in Google Forms. This will be a Google Form incorporating your story ending suggestions and offering your teammates the chance to suggest their own before getting crowdsourced feedback from your larger audience of readers.

To create your form, first log into `https://google.com`.

> **Note**
>
> When working with Google, make sure to get help from a family member or guardian if you are under 13 and need to be added to a family plan. Information on how to do this can be found at `http://support.google.com/accounts/answer/1350409`.

Once logged in, visit `http://docs.google.com/forms` and click the big **+** button to create a new blank form. The form that you are creating is intended to poll your teammates about the best ending to build. Give your form a title and description in the top box, then start filling out the multiple choice space in the form-builder box below.

Work with your initial brainstorm of the various endings that could happen in your story, adding each of them as a choice. Give your teammates the ability to provide their own ideas for an ending by clicking **add "other"** to add an **Other** option to the list of choices. Make this question required by choosing the **Required** toggle at the bottom right. Your form will resemble Figure 19.3, probably with other story ending possibilities.

Now, you're ready to send this form to your teammates. There are a couple of ways to do this. First, click the **Send** button at the top-right corner of the form builder screen. A pop-up window opens, and you can choose whether to send the form via an email, a link, or as embedded HTML. You probably have your team's email addresses, so add these addresses to the **Email > to** area of the pop-up window and click **Send**. Add a note in the message box of the pop-up to encourage them to add their own ending concepts and to reply by a certain date. Soon, you'll have a good idea of some possible endings for your story.

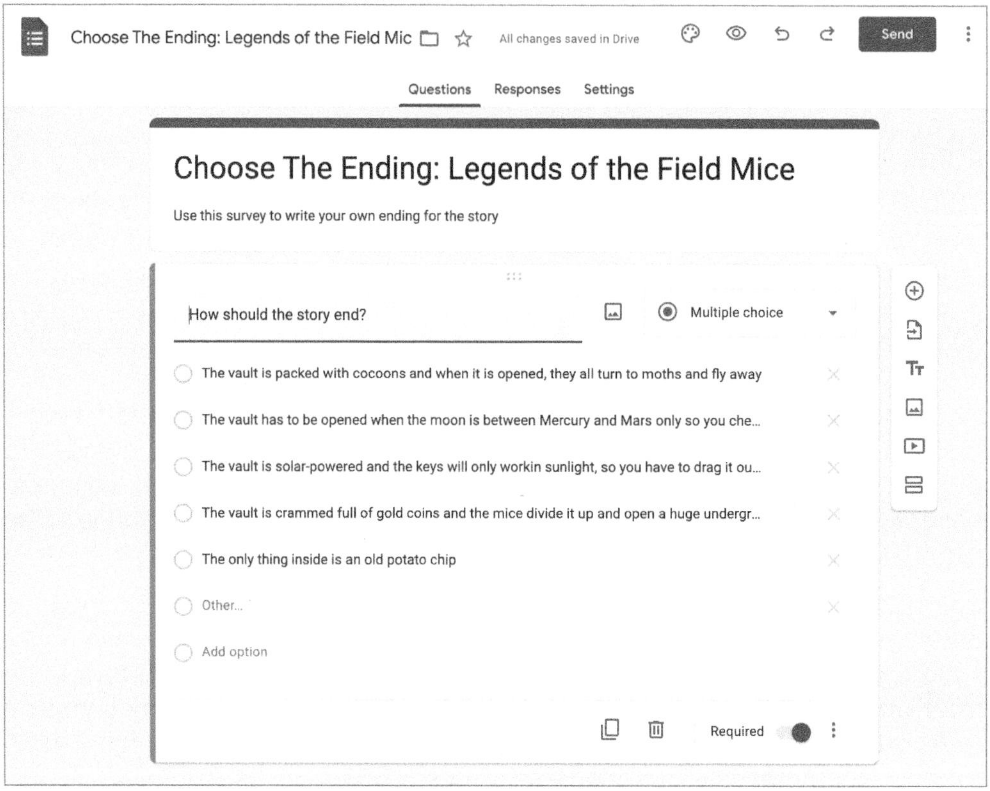

FIGURE 19.3: The first form to get ideas
Credit: Google LLC

Step 3: Create a Voting Form

Once your team has answered, go to `http://docs.google.com/forms` if you don't have it open and reopen your form. You can access the responses from the Responses tab, where you can see a summary chart of your responses as shown in Figure 19.4.

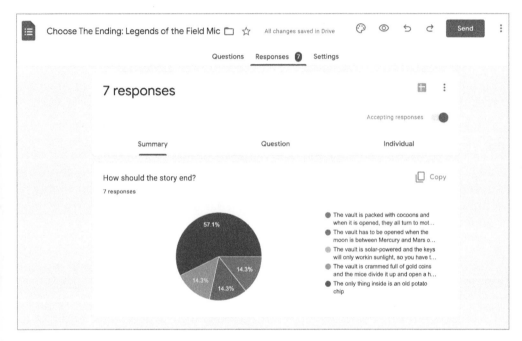

FIGURE 19.4: Your first form's responses
Credit: Google LLC

Now, you need to put all the ideas that you have gathered to a vote. Work with your team to pick the top three or four best story choices. Probably your team has come up with some excellent ideas, so pick a small number, including the most popular suggestions, and a few new ones that you all like best.

Create a second form with a voting option that you'll send out to a larger group of respondents. This form will have a rating mechanism for each idea. Build your form by editing its name and purpose at the top. You can call the form **Idea Evaluation** and explain its purpose by adding text similar to the following:

> *We need your help to pick the best ending for our story! Play through the story "Legends of the Field Mice" found at* `https://fir-shell-ambulance.glitch.me`*, and then vote on your favorite way to open the vault.*

> **Note**
>
> Edit the link to the story in your note for this new group of users to reflect your published story.

You can then edit the multiple choice box below to create a linear scale for each ending. Give the ratings a label so that 1 is the **Worst** idea and 5 is the **Best** idea. Make the question required to answer by sliding the Required toggle to the right. Your form should look like Figure 19.5 after entering the first option for an ending.

Add the final ending options to your form by clicking the button with the + sign on the right, adding an area for each question. Select **Linear Scale** in each drop-down to add a scale to each question, similar to the way you added your first question. Your final form will resemble Figure 19.6. This is a form designed to be disseminated far and wide, to get as many opinions on your endings as you can. Consider asking parents, their friends, other students, teachers, and relatives to play your story and give their crowdsourced opinion.

Once you get enough responses, you can discover the preferred ending suggested by your users. It's easier to do this by using the built-in spreadsheet capacity provided in Google Forms. Open your answers in a spreadsheet by going to the Responses tab in your Google Form and clicking the green button () at the top. A pop-up opens, asking how you want to open the spreadsheet. Choose the option to create a new Google Sheet and it will open with the possible endings listed as columns and the response votes recorded.

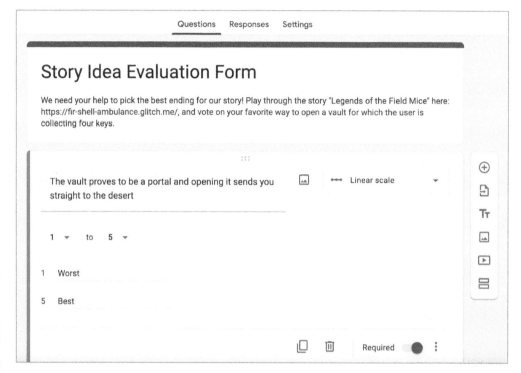

Story Idea Evaluation Form

We need your help to pick the best ending for our story! Play through the story "Legends of the Field Mice" here:
https://fir-shell-ambulance.glitch.me/, and vote on your favorite way to open a vault for which the user is
collecting four keys.

:::

The vault proves to be a portal and opening it sends you   •—•   Linear scale   ▾
straight to the desert

_____

1 ▾   to   5 ▾

1   Worst

5   Best

                                           Required ●   ⋮

FIGURE 19.5: Building your second Google Form
Credit: Google LLC.

Select the responses in each column and click the **Functions** button ($\sum$ ▾) on
the right at the top of the spreadsheet. Choose **SUM** and the sum of the votes
will appear in a new row under the data, as shown in Figure 19.7. This way, you
can more quickly get a tally of the votes.

Finally, you have the guidance you need to build the last part of your story: the
ending! Now, it's time to build the final scene of your story.

Step 4: Complete the Story

It's assumed that you've built the four passages of the story with the capacity
for the voyager to collect four keys.

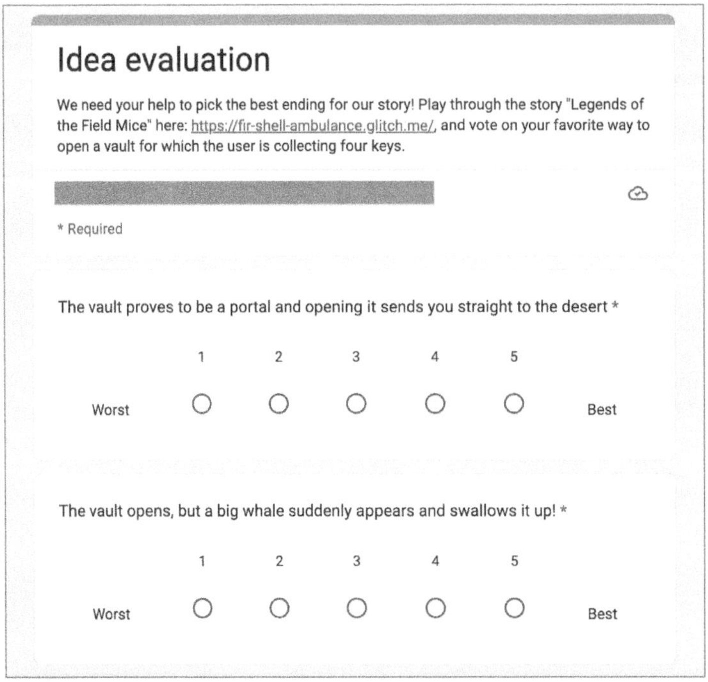

FIGURE 19.6: A view of the second Google Form
Credit: Google LLC

> **Note**
>
> If you built your story line a different way, that's fine, but you'll want to find a way for all the keys to match passage links. Your main goal is to build a satisfying ending to the story whereby all keys can be collected to arrive at the end result.

Now enhance the main tunnel's code to complete the story line:

- Only show passage links if a key has not been collected.
- Only show a passage to a vault if all four keys are in place.

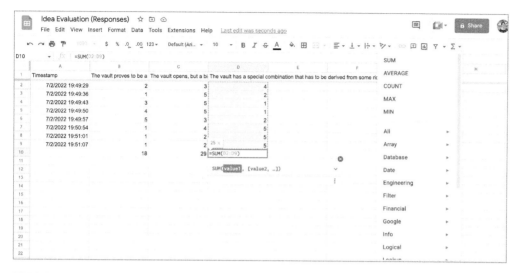

FIGURE 19.7: Tallying the votes in a Google Sheet

Credit: Google LLC

Edit the **Into the tunnel** passage with some conditional statements:

```
(unless:$keys contains "a black key")[[Go north]]
(unless:$keys contains "a red key")[[Go south]]
(unless:$keys contains "a green key")[[Go east]]
(unless:$keys contains "a blue key")[[Go west]]

(if:$keys's length is 4)
   [You've collected the four keys to the mysterious
vault, and now you are ready to see if you can open it.
   [[Go to the vault]]
]
```

This code specifies that a passage link will display if its corresponding key exists in inventory. If all four keys are collected, the vault passage opens.

Now, input the story line that your userbase preferred. We opted for something like the following to add to the new **Go to the vault** passage:

The mice squeak excitedly. Even the Mayor, usually unflap-
pable, is breathing heavily.
Finally, you will get to open the vault that has been
closed for so many years.

You examine the locks closely. There are faint traces of
paint on each keyhole. You
insert the keys in the color corresponding to the paint
flakes in each keyhole.

Squeakily, the locks each turn in sequence.

The door creaks open and you peer inside.

At the very bottom of the vault is a very old potato chip.

The mice all exhale a sigh of disappointment. The Mayor
picks it up and holds it up to the torchlight. "That's
it?" he says.

Suddenly, the spider that you chased away earlier descends
on a thread from the ceiling
of the tunnel and deftly plucks the potato chip from the
Mayor's fingers. "So that's
where that's been. I've been looking for this for years.
Thanks!" it says, munching the
potato chip happily. At least someone is pleased.

It's time to [[go home->Under the earth]] after this
fiasco. You exit the tunnel, no wiser than you were when
you came in.

Of course, your own users and team probably made up an ending that's far less
disappointing! Add it **to this area** and export your story one more time, adding
the final version to Glitch by overwriting your previous work. You can send your
users this final version to show them your work!

Extend Your Knowledge

In this chapter and the previous ones, you built a story line based on working as a team and via a larger, anonymous, crowdsourced input. This *participatory engineering* is a good way to meet your users, customers, and clients where they are and bring them into the process of creation. With luck and a healthy amount of input, crowdsourcing is a great way to build, launch, rebuild, and relaunch products.

Not every crowdsourcing story ends well, however. Read the case study in the *Harvard Business Review* by visiting `hbr.org/2016/12/a-case-study-of-crowdsourcing-gone-wrong`. In this example, a company called Quirky is shown to have failed in part because of its reliance on crowdsourcing. The company was not able to launch a truly groundbreaking product, releasing instead dozens of good, but not great, products spanning many categories. Do you think that your democratic approach to choosing the ending of your story created the best experience for your players? Why or why not?

Vocabulary Review

In your own words, describe:

- Explicit feedback
- Feedback mechanisms
- Implicit feedback

Quiz

The following quiz questions are to test your knowledge of the material presented in this chapter. Select the best answer for each of the following:

Q1: Crowdsourcing always provides the best feedback.
  a. True
  b. False

Q2: Implicit feedback can be:
   a. In the form of analytics
   b. Added to a website behind the scenes
   c. Both of these
Q3: Explicit feedback can be:
   a. Analytics
   b. Email lists
   c. A survey widget

Assignment: A Postmortem

Now that your story is complete, make sure the latest version is published and send it back to all the folks who gave you feedback initially on its form and ending. What do they think? Gather three of the most interesting comments they make and write a postmortem, or an analysis, of what you would do differently in a similar project following this one. Use the worksheet at `CS4Kids.com/assets/ch19-worksheet.pdf` for useful prompts.

20. The Real World

Standard: 2-IC-20: Compare tradeoffs associated with computing technologies that affect people's everyday activities and career options

As you emerge from your adventure underground, miraculously growing back to your original height, you reflect on the challenges you've faced over the past days and the progress you've made in learning how to address them. You created machines in support of fireflies and prototyped protective enclosures to surround rare moss species. You built a 3D world to envision ways of protecting a grove of petrified wood and dabbled in data science and databases to build a circulating library for visitors to safely study the interesting stones that gather in the stream. Finally, you created a winding story online for others to learn the hidden narratives that the field mice wanted the world to know. Congratulations on your accomplishments!

As you bid goodbye to your Guide and walk home, you think about how you might translate the work you have done in this forest to help human populations. What kind of app, story, game, or data science could you use that might help in the "real," human-focused world? Could your project fill a gap that has been caused by the digitization of the world?

Do Some Research

Software infuses the world around us, and while software is still "eat(ing) the world" by disrupting older, more established technologies, as Marc Andreeson said in 2011 (`https://a16z.com/2011/08/20/why-software-is-eating-the-world`), by disrupting older, more established technologies, it is also disrupting society. The use of GPS, for example, disrupted the use of paper maps for navigation. Spotify has disrupted the music industry, and TikTok has disrupted marketing. As new applications are built to support various industries, older processes fall by the wayside as computers take over more manual tasks. As artificial intelligence increasingly infuses software applications to make them ever "smarter," it is causing the next wave of disruption as it uncovers previously undiscovered patterns in data.

This march toward the digitization of all things previously done manually has had far-reaching social consequences. Some jobs have been eliminated because they have been rendered obsolete. Consider the travel industry, for example. Previously, it was common to visit a travel agent after deciding to take a trip. The travel agent would help arrange all the details. Nowadays, an Internet search and a few clicks are all it takes to book an entire vacation. As the Internet brings buyers and sellers together, it has also caused some chaos as industries and individuals rush to adapt to the new norms of doing business. In addition, a digital divide has been created among those communities with less access to Internet and communications resources and thus less connected to these disruptive technologies.

Research the positive and negative aspects of our increasingly digital existence. Think about how your own experience of school has changed over the past few years as your classrooms have embraced the digitized world. Consider an industry as large as agriculture or as small as the household lighting industry, for example. How has software helped farmers use water more efficiently, detect diseases in livestock, or address climate change in their locations? On the flip side, how has this digitization of agriculture impacted smaller farmers compared to larger industrial farms? How has the invention of Wi-Fi-connected smart lighting made the experience of managing a home's atmosphere more interesting, efficient, and delightful? How has this invention impacted factory workers who have been building incandescent versus LED lighting? How has the proliferation of software jobs, in general, impacted industries that rely on skilled electrical and mechanical engineers, rather than software engineers?

Your Challenge

One way that concerned technologists have addressed potential harms caused by the increasing prevalence of software in industries has been to build socially conscious coding practices as well as applications that address specific social concerns. Coding for social good is a goal of many foundations, startups, and even segments of the largest companies in the world, such as Google and Microsoft. For example, Google Arts and Culture (`http://artsandculture.google.com/partner`) has worked to bring museums into your home.

308

Microsoft's AI for Earth programs (www.microsoft.com/ai/ai-for-earth) offer many different solutions to address wildlife and earth science challenges worldwide. Your challenge is to use the skills that you learned in this textbook and create an app for social good that addresses something that you see happening in your community or home.

Sketch It Out

Brainstorm a topic that you think could be helped by building a software solution to address it. It can be a small idea like cataloging the veteran graves in your local cemetery, a medium idea like creating a mental health app for your school, or a big idea like helping all the stray pets in your country find forever homes. Maybe your idea can be inspired by the United Nation's AI for Good Sustainable Development Goals (www.un.org/en/sustainable-development-goals) listed in Figure 20.1.

FIGURE 20.1: The 17 UN Sustainable Development Goals, from www.un.org/en/sustainable-development-goals
Source: MintBlak/Adobe Stock

As you brainstorm, keep in mind the effect that your app might have on broader social groups than the ones you are targeting, and note these potential effects—good and bad—in your sketch. Your brainstorming might look like Figure 20.2.

FIGURE 20.2: Brainstorming social good projects

Think Like a Computer Scientist

Computer scientists focused on building software for social good need to look at the topics they are trying to address and build software with these in mind. When building a website, for example, engineers should begin by considering accessibility topics so that every person will be able to use the site, regardless of ability. When building the software that powers a nonprofit foundation, engineers should be particularly aware of costs incurred for hosting, database storage, and other financial considerations that impact a nonprofit's often-lean budget. When building a "green" solution, it is imperative that engineers think about the electricity used to host their software solution.

For this reason, groups such as the Green Software Foundation have formed to help engineers consider many of these topics from the ground up. Read through `https://principles.green` to discover the ways that sustainable software can be developed. Maybe these considerations can help you engineer your own software more sustainably.

Project Recipes

This project section will not encompass one single recipe for one app, but rather give ideas about how you can use the skills you gathered by working through the projects in this book. The following sections contain five possible applications you could do. These are:

- Clean Up Your Town
- Get Fit
- Convince Your Parents to Get a Cat or Dog
- Build an Art Gallery
- Build an Elder's Story

In each of the following sections, you will be presented with considerations on how you might build the solution to one of these applications using MakeCode, Micro:bit, A-Frame, data science with Kaggle, or Twine. Each section contains a good, better, and best section to give you an idea of where to start and how you can scale your project.

Project 1: Clean Up Your Town with MakeCode

Does it feel like your town could use a tidy-up? Do you see litter on the roads or in the parks? Use the skills you acquired building a game with MakeCode Arcade in Chapters 4–6.

Good: Make a map in MakeCode of an area of your town or neighborhood, drawing the streets, parks, and major buildings in a tilemap. Indicate the areas that you think should be cleaned up, much like OpenLitterMap (`http://open-littermap.com`).

Better: Make this experience more useful by building it as a multiplayer game using the MakeCode controller blocks. You can make a multiplayer game where the players who pick up or capture the most pieces of litter in the game get the highest score. Some sample code can be found in the MakeCode documentation at `http://arcade.makecode.com/courses/csintro2/logic/multiplayer` and a sample multiplayer game can be found at `http://arcade.makecode.com/50683-88990-99209-03861`.

Best: Make the game even more real by building the sample game based on user input from OpenLitterMap in your town. You can build a team to log the litter on OpenLitterMap based on their observations in their neighborhoods, then build game challenges for the town sections that have the most litter. Create mini litter challenges so that the user who loses a game in MakeCode is tasked with picking up and disposing of the litter in the actual area of town where it was discovered. The good news is that even if the loser of the game must pick up litter, they will be able to get a reward such as Littercoin from OpenLitterMap and might help get your team on a leaderboard, so they win after all. This is also a moment when you can practice your crowdsourcing skills, acquired in Chapter 17, "The Field Mice."

Project 2: Get Fit with Micro:bit

Sitting around all day scrolling through social media isn't a healthy activity. Can you challenge yourself and your friends to be more active? Why not use your knowledge of working with the micro:bit from Chapters 1–3 for better fitness?

Good: If you can get access to a physical micro:bit, perhaps in an online store such as AdaFruit (`www.adafruit.com`) and a battery pack to power it, you can attach it to your leg, ankle, or shoe and program its accelerometer to count your steps. Make a step counter using the tutorial found at `www.microbit.org/projects/make-it-code-it/step-counter` or the tutorial found at `www.microbit.org/projects/make-it-code-it/sensitive-step-counter` (which uses a more sensitive motion sensor). The accelerometer will be able to detect a "shake" kind of movement and determine how many steps you take in a day.

Better: Partner with other micro:bit owners, maybe in your family, school, or community, and create a challenge website where people can input how many steps they take daily. Build a leaderboard and have a weekly award for the person who tops a leaderboard. You could even bring this challenge to your pets and see if you can determine how many steps your dogs take on their walks, to give a prize to the fittest pet!

Best: Determine, based on data sent from the accelerometer, whether you can differentiate between a jump, skip, hop, step, or stride. Create a movement sequence game where a web application, maybe using MakeCode, determines a fast step sequence that users must match, similar to dance games like Dance Revolution. Who can top the leaderboard and prove their fancy footwork with the micro:bit?

Project 3: Convince Your Parents to Get a Pet Using Data Science

Did you ever try to convince your parents or guardian that you really need a cat or a dog? What if you could use data science to create a truly data-driven approach to convince them that you need a new pet? Flex your data wrangling muscles as you did in Chapters 9–11 when creating the rock library. Now that you have worked with Kaggle to build charts and graphs and to analyze datasets, you can.

Good: Use the dataset at `www.kaggle.com/datasets/valchovalev/cat-vs-dog-popularity-in-us` or some other dataset to build up a notebook and explain to your parents that, in your region, you should adopt either a cat or a dog because, depending on your state, cats or dogs are more or less popular (so the less popular animal might be more prevalent in shelters).

Better: Compare the results of your analysis of this dataset and correlate it with local pets on `PetFinder.com` that are up for adoption. Build a website explaining how the data shows that a particular trend in pet popularity correlates to similar data on PetFinder regarding the pets that are available in your area.

Best: Create your own dataset from `PetFinder.com`'s free API found at `www.petfinder.com/developers`. You can source your own dataset and import it into your notebook as you did to categorize rocks. This time, you'll categorize pets by their size, energy level, fur type, and other characteristics, and create a truly customized explanation about why a particular pet is perfect for your home, based on data science!

Project 4: Build an Art Gallery with A-Frame

Now that you've built a web app in Glitch using A-Frame in Chapters 13–15, you can use this tool to bring experiences to users, rather than expecting people to travel to view experiences. Build a facsimile of a famous art museum gallery in A-Frame and show it to someone who has never been to the museum.

Good: You could, for example, re-create the famous series of Monet's water lily paintings that encircle the Orangerie Museum's gallery. You can see this series of paintings at `www.musee-orangerie.fr/en/node/197502`.

Better: Create your own private art gallery, with your own art or sculptures displayed in your A-Frame world. Invite your friends and family to view the art.

Best: Create a community art show, inviting a group to submit their works to your gallery space. Invite everyone to narrate their works by providing show notes. If possible, provide your guests with a headset viewer such as Google Cardboard (`http://arvr.google.com/cardboard/get-cardboard`) for a more immersive experience, to allow guests to wander through the space on their own.

Project 5: Build an Elder's Story with Twine

You've built a fantasy story about a mysterious vault that has puzzled generations of field mice, but how could you use Twine for a more real world application?

Good: Interview an older member of your family, community, or school. Can you create a story that echoes something that happened during their life?

The winding nature of Twine stories can work to re-create the various decisions that this person made during their life and even help them envision and recall the ramifications of their decisions.

Better: Work with two members of your family, perhaps a grandmother and a grandfather, to tell the story of a common experience such as a family trip. How do their differing points of view inform the storyline? Use Twine to re-create the various decisions that were made before and during the experience. Ask them to imagine how the experience might have changed had other decisions been made, and document it in the Twine story. Make sure to preserve their unique vocabulary and expressions to retain their voices.

Best: Work with a team to build and export a library of elder stories and collate them into a website, grouping them as you find common themes such as World War II stories, stories about your town, or immigrant narratives. Talk to your local library about whether you can find a place to archive your stories as part of your local narrative.

Extend Your Knowledge

You've used this time to build a useful and innovative interactive experience, perhaps to tell stories, clean up your environment, or get fitter. All these socially aware applications are built to solve an issue that you've seen in your community or enhance someone's life by building software in support of their needs. Not all software that is built for social purposes is necessarily good, however. Even if intentions are good, sometimes the results can be damaging to communities. A good example is the creation of facial recognition technologies.

While it's an easy shortcut to use facial recognition for security tasks, such as to unlock a phone screen, these technologies can also be misused—for example, to profile people as potential criminals simply based on their facial expressions. Do some research about the harms that can be caused by the unwise creation of some software. A good place to start is Microsoft's Responsible AI landing page at `www.microsoft.com/en-us/ai/responsible-ai-resources`, which contains links for many projects designed to mitigate the harms of unfair AI practices. Research other ways that companies are making their software projects more ethical, fair, and harmless.

Vocabulary Review

In your own words, describe:

- Coding for social good
- Digitization
- Harms

Quiz

The following quiz questions are to test your knowledge of the material presented in this chapter. Select the best answer for each of the following:

Q1: Software development is always built with ethical considerations baked in.
   a. True
   b. False

Q2: The Green Software Foundation focuses on:
   a. Software development for agriculture
   b. Software development for landscape design
   c. How to build software with sustainability in mind

Q3: Software for social good is rarely found in the real world.
   a. True
   b. False

Assignment: Demo Day

In this chapter, you built a project that uses the skills you learned throughout this book. Now you can show it off! Work with your town library, your local school club, or a different group in your community to have a "demo day" where you and your friends can show what you have built. Ask the audience for tips on how you can make it better, and then iterate your design. The story is yours to tell!

Index

318

320